7 Steps

to

Better

Writing

7 Steps to Better Writing

How to write better reports, proposals, email, blogs, and web content

Charles Maxwell

TOWERING SKILLS LLC

Edition 1.02

Published by
Towering Skills LLC, Queen Creek, Arizona
www.toweringskills.com

ISBN 978-1-7314-6488-0

Table of Contents

What You Will Learn

This book will help you write better, faster, and with more ease and confidence. The ability to write well is essential to your success.

Much of what we read today is poorly written. This seems to make it acceptable to disregard how you write. But this is not true. Poorly written documents are ignored, only partly read, or misunderstood.

You know this. Your email inbox is full of unwanted and irrelevant sales copy. At your job, you are expected to read manuals, reports, and contracts that are long-winded and impenetrable. It is slow reading and hard thinking. And there is a lot of it.

This type of material brings with it mental discomfort every time you have to engage with it. The fog causes lost productivity, lost support, and lost sales.

Moreover, if what other people write is so bad, what can you say about your own writing? Is it more of the same? A murky miasma?

What if it were clear, concise, and engaging? What could you accomplish if what you wrote stood out like a brilliant neon sign in a dark night?

If what you write is not as succinct and engrossing as you would like, then this book is for you. This slim volume will show you how to capture and keep the attention of your readers. It will deliver the insights you need to write with skill.

This book is the outgrowth of my own long journey to improve my writing as an engineer, analyst, manager, and ghostwriter. A dozen years ago, I assembled what I had learned into a short course and coaching practice. That work eventually resulted in this book. People with decades of professional experience—as well as those just out of high school and college—have benefited by learning and using the principles shared here.

If you use my 7-step writing process, I know your writing will improve. You will be able to:

- Capture the attention of your readers
- Save time collecting the facts needed to support your writing projects

- Frame your thoughts quickly
- Develop convincing arguments
- Compose with speed
- Cut out the fat that keeps people from reading your material
- Produce engaging documents that achieve results
- Be more confident

Furthermore, you will learn how to leverage the latest electronic technology to do more with less effort. Be assured—there is a lot more to this than spelling and grammar checking.

One other point. This book covers 99% of what you need to know to write well, yet the book has less than 40,000 words. There is no other resource this comprehensive and concise.

Applying these principles will help you write with brevity, clarity, efficacy, and power.

Let's get started.

Good Writing Is Important

Effective writing drives the success of individuals and organizations. Well-written documents achieve better results and save time. Some experts estimate that poor writing costs the US economy $400 billion each year. Given this information, the annual global cost of poor writing surely tops $1 trillion.

But, poor writing does more than waste money. It also fosters misunderstanding, damages relationships, and wastes human potential.

While most people are unconcerned about the aggregate loss, we each are acutely aware of our own disappointments and pain. Sales are lost by poorly written proposals and ineffective sales copy. Careers are stunted by weak writing skills. In addition, all of us have been frustrated by confusing instructions and angered by harsh internet posts and insensitive emails.

Tom Peters says, "The quality of written communication is still incredibly important.... Work on your writing. It is a timeless and powerful skill."[1]

Good writers in business, government, technology, the sciences, education, sports, the arts, religion, and charities know they need to understand their audience and customize their messages to specific interests. They work to understand their readers' needs, to deliver useful information, and to motivate action.

Documents Are the Bridges We Build to Convey Our Thoughts

Like builders needing to construct bridges to cross rivers, writers face the challenge of spanning gulfs of misunderstanding and ignorance. The documents they create are bridges to knowledge and trust.

Bridges are designed before they are built. Engineers first think through what will work best for each location and transportation need. Similarly, writers must determine what ideas are required for each situation and how to express those thoughts. Often, writers discover how to state an idea only by venturing forth with a rough draft, revising it many times—striving, at each step, to be concrete, brief, and fair, and only then gradually articulating elusive thoughts. As writers labor to make their ideas clear, their messages take form like the steel and concrete spanning out across deep water. In this way, clear writing becomes clear thinking—with clarity abiding both in the writer and in readers.

Abraham Lincoln was an effective writer who planned his compositions and thoroughly revised his work.

Consider Abraham Lincoln. He spent much effort drafting and editing the Gettysburg Address, which includes only 270 words.[2] He was concerned about the national audience—not just those who would gather on 19 November 1863 at a new cemetery in Pennsylvania. He knew that journalists would latch on to his words and that millions of newspaper-reading citizens would reflect on his remarks.

Lincoln wanted his words to serve for more than a personal comment on the day's program. He hoped to comfort those who had lost

4

family and friends. Furthermore, he sought to persuade the nation to continue to make the sacrifices required to win the war and to reunite the nation.

Being thus highly motivated, he worked hard to determine what to say and how to say it. His effort was not wasted. Indeed, his words continue to stir the hearts of people throughout the world.

Your writing too can create bridges of understanding and persuasion.

Clear Writing Improves Thinking

Marvin H. Swift, a professor at the General Motors Institute at Flint, Michigan, in an article for *Harvard Business Review*, showed the link between writing and thinking.[3] Swift described a manager upset because many employees were using the company's copy machine for "personal matters, income tax forms, church programs, children's term papers," and more.

Determined to stop what he felt was an abuse of company assets, the manager dashed off a harsh directive threatening employees with termination if they continued to make photocopies for personal use. However, before distributing the memo, the manager reviewed his work and realized what he had written was not the message he wanted to send. He started revising the document to eliminate wordiness and to make the instructions clearer. As he progressed, he realized his note was too harsh, so he changed a few words to soften the tone. As he did this, he recognized that the logic underlying his memo was flawed. With this insight, the manager began to rethink his logic, and in doing this, he articulated a different policy—a guideline that would allow employees to pay for and self-police copies made for personal use. Through these rewrites, the manager found a better solution.

What is true for memos and short emails is even more valid for contracts, proposals, plans, technical articles, presentations, and other complicated documents. Complex and important documents benefit from iterative preparation.

This type of effort is not limited to big organizations and expensive projects. It also applies to individuals and smaller efforts. Most of us can recall starting to compose an email or letter, having to lay it aside, and later taking it up again and then seeing how what we wrote earlier needed fixing.

Turning ideas into words and putting those words down on paper or up on a computer screen allows us to reencounter our own ideas and imagine how others will receive them. As we reconsider what we wrote, we learn from our writing.

This is not a new phenomenon. Since the earliest times, teachers have required their students to compose and rewrite documents to help their students master what they were studying.

In general, the best writing requires the hardest thinking. This hard thinking goes by such labels as analyzing, diagnosing, planning, and pondering. Facets of this thought process include:

- Anticipating the readers' needs and their reactions
- Collecting and organizing facts
- Selecting what to say and what to leave unsaid
- Fusing small ideas into a larger meaning
- Crafting persuasive arguments
- Conveying the right feeling

Good Writing Has Always Been Important

Large organizations have always required documents. Ancient cultures invented prose thousands of years ago to communicate complicated thoughts, to reach people at a distance, and to preserve ideas.

For millennia, people have communicated by writing, as seen by this Sumerian cuneiform clay tablet from 2500 BC, which is an accounting report on silver assets.

As the world has progressed, it has become more complex, and the need for clear writing has increased. In the 21st Century, as technology rushes forward and as trade and communication reaches every part of the globe, effective writing grows even more valuable.

The Modern World Depends on Writing

More and more people are using the internet to receive and to provide information. This is rapidly expanding the amount of written material, and it is increasing the importance of distinguishing what you write. If you want to reach people, you need to write material that stands out from the crowd.

The number of published books now exceeds 200 million volumes. More than 2 million bloggers daily make a post. In addition, the horde of internal unpublished documents is gigantic.

In addition, there is email. During 2017, 2.7 billion people sent 269 billion emails each day, of which 50% were non-spam. This equates to 50 non-spam emails per day per person. And many people receive more.[4]

This is a lot of reading.

Furthermore, the majority of managers and professional employees today are knowledge workers—their job is managing information. Consequently, many professionals spend a large part of their time writing or reading documents. Business letters, reports, presentations, specifications, price quotations, webpages, and plans consume many hours as workers research, draft, revise, rewrite, and proof documents, and as readers read and act on those documents.

Even when people are watching or listening to movies, television, radio, internet videos, podcasts, music, lectures, and sermons, almost all of that content starts with the written word. People have to write it to keep it straight.

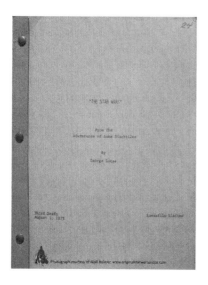

Movies, videos, radio programs, and podcasts require writing, as seen by this script for the first Star Wars movie.

Writing Better Can Boost Your Career

Few people have been fired because they wrote poorly. However, many business and technical people have been passed over for promotions, because they failed to write well. Most people in commerce, industry, and government have been frustrated to see at least some of their ideas be ignored, some of their work go unnoticed, or some of their projects be left unfunded. Many of those failures are rooted in failed communications.

We all have encountered emails or internet posts that created the wrong tone—hurting feelings and generating resentment. In addition, much sales copy fails to capture the attention of clients, and many technical, legal, and financial documents are ignored, because they are overly complicated, confusing, or incomplete. If we are the authors of these offending or neglected documents, then we are apt to suffer the fallback.

On the other hand, those who rise to the challenge of writing well enjoy recognition and other rewards. A few instances I have witnessed include:

- A middle manager, with only a high school education, moved into upper management, because he could write well. His organization skills and work ethic were excellent, but his writing skills set him apart from other employees.

- A young intern at a large company received praise from a vice president across the country, because the intern wrote reports that clearly communicated information important to the firm.

- An engineer always found herself in demand, because she wrote thoroughly researched and data-rich reports on complex topics.

- An engineer lost his job in industry during an economic downturn, but rapidly found employment in an important federal agency, because he wrote exceptionally well.

- A young professional was retained by his company when the industry slipped into a deep economic recession causing the discharge of thousands of employees, because management valued the person's writing ability.

- A senior manager, who had many enemies in the company, avoided being fired for many years, because the company's president relied upon the person to ghostwrite sensitive documents.

- A senior professional, in spite of her having physical health limitations, was called back from retirement, because management prized the woman's towering writing skills.

Superior writing skills are helpful to gaining and retaining management responsibility. Capturing ideas and decisions in typed words conveys a person's intellectual strength and managerial capability. A person's writing proficiency shows others your ability to think, organize, and communicate.

This is particularly important for young professionals who have not yet established their reputations. Lacking direct access to higher levels of management, a young worker can gain attention by producing superb documents. A well-crafted report or white paper can travel through even the most bureaucratic organization and display the person's thinking to high-ranking leaders. Therefore, it is no surprise that writing well is a vehicle to being recognized.

Conclusion

Good writing always has been and always will be important. In our information-rich society, clear and tight writing indicates a perceptive mind and a disciplined approach to productivity. Embracing these skills will improve your career.

Additional Resources

For videos and more information on the importance of writing, go to: www.toweringskills.com/7steps/more/.

7-Step Writing Process

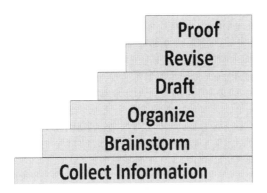

Proof
Revise
Draft
Organize
Brainstorm
Collect Information

It has been said that the secret of getting ahead is getting started, and the secret of getting started is breaking a complex job into smaller tasks, and then starting on the first one and moving on to the last.[5] Extensive research shows this maxim applies to writing. The best way to write good material is to:

1. Identify your *readers* and your *purpose*.
2. *Collect* the facts needed to support your message.
3. *Brainstorm*. Creatively look for thoughts that support your purpose. Be open to new ideas, and work rapidly to generate and capture your thoughts.
4. *Organize* your ideas. Determine the main concepts and supporting details. Place them in a logical order.
5. Rapidly *draft* the text, using the materials from steps 1-4.
6. *Revise* your draft to refine the logic, enhance the structure, improve the flow, and choose the best words. This is also called editing.
7. *Proof* your document.

Steps 1-4 are *prewriting* stages. Effective prewriting eliminates writer's block, helps you compose text rapidly, keeps you on track, and minimizes the need to revise what you draft. Not knowing how to prewrite often is the root cause of people's dislike for writing and their poor results when they do.

All the writing steps are essential. Generally, collecting material (step 2) and revising (step 6) require the most time, while the most technically challenging phase is editing (step 6).

Sequencing the discrete tasks is important. Too often, in an effort to quickly be done with it, people start composing before they are ready. Rushing into the drafting step without preparation lengthens the job, increases the effort, and degrades the product. On the other hand, making ample preparation speeds the total process, reduces the strain, and yields better results.

So, start with the first step and then advance one step at a time. As you proceed, you may need to revert to an earlier phase. This is OK, because often your progress will reveal things that alter your earlier assumptions. Indeed, such learning is unavoidable and beneficial.

Your Personal Plan

You will gain the most from this book, if, at the end of each chapter, you pause to consider what you have learned and plan to apply it. This will help you make quicker progress.

To help you reflect on the key principles, you will find questions at the end of each chapter. Answer each question by writing or typing your response.

What do you feel you should do to improve your writing?

What is the best way for you to achieve this goal?

Additional Resources

For videos and more information on writing as a process, go to: www.toweringskills.com/7steps/more/.

Step 1 – Identify Readers & Purpose

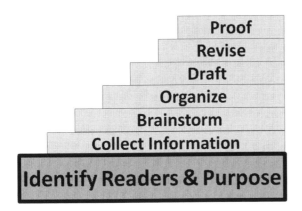

The first step to good writing is to gain a clear understanding of your readers and your message.

Here is why. You do not want to work hard on a lengthy report or complex proposal, only to see it go unread or its recommendations ignored. You also do not want to write an email and later realize that the substance or tone was wrong. Yet this is what can happen if you misjudge your audience and their needs. You can avoid missteps if you get clear on your readers, understand their desires, and match your messages to their situations.

Seek Guidance

When starting on a new writing assignment seek guidance from your sponsor, your supervisor, a topic expert, or some of your readers. Probe for understanding and make notes. Your notes will prove helpful as you advance your project.

Put Yourself in the Place of Your Readers

When writing factual material, you need to know who your readers are, or at least imagine who they might be. If your audience is indistinct, your message will be vague or inappropriate.

Ask the questions:

- Who wants me to write this?
- Who will read it?
- Are my readers looking for a solution to a problem? Are they seeking an explanation, justification, affirmation, consolation, or something else?
- What do my readers think and feel?

Define Your Purpose

After you understand your readers, define your purpose. Your purpose will have a topic and a theme. Your topic is the subject—what you want to discuss. Your theme—also called the thesis or premise—is your opinion on the topic or the meaning of the topic. As you define your purpose, ask:

- What do I hope to accomplish?
- What do I want my readers to know or think?
- What do I want them to feel?
- What do I want them to do?

Limit yourself to one topic, and determine your opinion of the topic. For example, if writing about software, the topic would be the type of software, and a possible theme could be your contention that the software is easy to use, widely available, and appropriate to your department's needs. An alternative theme might be that the software is hard to use, limited to a few users, and therefore unsuitable.

It is normal to have to invest effort into fully identifying your message. Furthermore, perfecting your understanding generally requires an iterative approach of articulating part of your purpose and then learning more. If you have limited knowledge of your readership or only have a vague understanding of your material, start with what you know and expand your understanding through research and brainstorming. As you proceed, continue to visualize your readers and anticipate how they will react to your message. As you do, you will become more aware of points to make and ways to express them.

Write or Not Write

As you define your purpose, you may decide not to write. Instances when you should not write include:

- Not having anything to say
- Not knowing the facts
- Being the wrong person to write
- Risking too much

If you cannot identify a purpose for your document, then you are wasting your time. Journalists, bloggers, and newsletter authors have to find something worthwhile to say. If they do not, their writing is unfocused, and they will lose readership. If you do not know what to say, you too will fail to write well.

If you are struggling to clarify your purpose, a way to discover one is to identify a problem and then provide a solution. Another approach is to discuss what is new or unusual.

In addition, if you do not know the facts, you should not write. Wait until you learn the particulars.

Writing also requires having the appropriate individual communicate at the appropriate time. Perhaps a different person in your organization needs to write—one with more knowledge, more authority, or less immediacy. Select the right person.

On other occasions, the time might be wrong. If it is untimely, wait.

Last of all, there are instances when writing is too risky. A written message can be too formal, too inflexible, or too dangerous. Customer dissatisfaction, personnel problems, and criticism are best handled face-to-face. These situations need flexibility and immediate feedback.

When you cannot anticipate your audience's initial position or their changing point of view as a conversation progresses, you will do better if you talk in person or use the phone. This allows you to modify your remarks to match the dynamics of the conversation.

Make Notes

It helps to list your readers and jot down their needs and concerns. Putting information down on paper or up on a computer screen improves thinking. As your audience and their needs come into better view, summarize your message in a few words.

Your notes need not be lengthy, but they need to be written so you can refer to them later.

Create an Attribute Matrix

If you have many different types of readers with complex needs, consider preparing an ***attribute matrix***. This is a table where the rows list readers or reader groups, the columns list attributes of those readers or groups, and the intersecting squares show scores that reflect the reader's interests or needs.

For example, if you were writing sales copy to influence potential smart phone customers, you could assign income groups to rows and customers' interests (such as modernity, functionality, and price) to columns. You could then score the intersecting rows and columns with numbers where low numbers represent low interest and high numbers represent high interest. You also could do this with age, education, location, etc.

Here is a simple example, where 0 (zero) represents no importance, 1 represents low importance, 2 represents moderate importance, and 3 represents high importance.

Customers' Income	Importance to Customers		
	Modernity	Function	Price
Low	0	2	3
Moderate	2	2	2
High	3	3	1

This method may provide little value to simple problems. However, complex situations benefit from this approach, because the tool helps prioritize what to emphasize.

For a complex topic, consider using the data from an attribute matrix to create a ***histogram*** (en.wikipedia.org/wiki/Histogram) or ***polar distribution chart*** (en.wikipedia.org/wiki/Radar_chart). Obviously, you will go to this trouble only if the writing project is highly important and complex.

The essential point is to characterize your readers and their needs.

Match Your Document's Form to Its Purpose

As you consider your purpose, define your scope. Determine how long your message should be. Will a one-paragraph email suffice? Alternatively, do you need a 100-page analysis? How important is it to preserve the message and the supporting information?

Simple questions generally call for simple responses. Conversely, complex inquiries and formal requests dictate more serious formats, such as reports, white papers, and proposals. In addition, consider how your readers will receive and use the information and its delivery vehicle.

Control the Tone

Tone is the mindset of the writer towards the reader. The writer's feelings influence the written word. The writer expresses tone by selecting events and details and by constructing sentences that reflect those feelings. This happens subconsciously. What flows out is tone—be it objective, biased, cheerful, sad, angry, cordial, serious, whimsical, open, guarded, a combination of any of these, or something entirely different. (You will find more information on tone in the chapter on writing step 5.)

What is important is to match your document's tone to its purpose. You will accomplish this by controlling how you feel about the topic and your readers. So, consider tone.

Summary

In conclusion, writing well starts with understanding your readers, identifying their needs, and determining a message. Laying this foundation will ensure that the rest of your work is productive.

Your Personal Plan

What documents do you need to write soon? Who will read those documents? What do your readers want or need to hear? How will you satisfy their needs?

On your next writing project, make a list of your readers and their needs. If your list is long and your readers' needs complex, prepare an attribute table showing the intersections of your readers and their needs. Use this list or table to guide your research and writing.

Additional Resources

For videos and more ideas on identifying your readers and understanding your purpose, go to: www.toweringskills.com/7steps/more/.

Step 2 – Collect Information

Much of what you will need to write will require more information than you possess when you begin. The challenge is to gather sufficient suitable material as fast as possible.

Consider Your Purpose

Collecting materials for a writing assignment starts with having a clear view of your readers and your scope. As you begin to gather information, ask:

- What material do I already have that I can use?
- What additional data would I like to have?
- What are the best sources for finding more material?
- How much time can I devote to research?
- What type of startling facts or stories should I target, which will attract attention and support my purpose?

Set a Goal

Decide how much time you can devote to research. If you are not specific, you easily can waste time learning interesting things, but not achieve your purpose promptly.

Make a research list and refer to it as you advance your project. Your plan should include:

- Questions to answer
- Topics to flesh out
- Milestone dates for completing phases of your research
- Likely sources
- Locations of those sources

Report Progress

As you advance your research, monitor your progress and periodically report to your sponsor (and, if appropriate, to your readers and other stakeholders). This will ensure that you stay oriented and make good use of your time and means. It also will help you gain buy-in and win approval of your completed project.

Be accountable. Focus on what is important. Research can be recreation, true; but if you have made a commitment to complete your assignment by a set time, then you must work on your task and not get distracted.

Sources

As you determine what evidence will best suit your purpose, consider where to find that information. Ask yourself:

- Do my readers expect to see evidence from primary or secondary sources? (Primary sources are those with immediate knowledge: experiments, observations, interviews, surveys, etc.; while secondary sources are distillations of primary sources.)
- What are the sources that I can most easily access that will supply the information I need?

Yourself

Start your research by determining what you already know on the topic and what resources you have in your immediate possession. Do this before expanding out.

Other People

Other people usually are your next best source of information. Talk to those who can directly supply information or who can direct you to other leads. Tap into coworkers, your professional network, suppliers, and customers.

Determine the experts who are accessible to you. Specialists can quickly provide information that would take you much longer to discover on your own.

Interviews

As you proceed, use good interviewing techniques. Here are tips for conducting interviews:

- Interview one person at a time. Group interviews are difficult to control and can easily get off track.

- In advance, make an appointment for the interview, even if the appointment is as little as 15 minutes ahead. This allows the interviewee to focus on the interview and avoid interruptions. In addition, it allows the interviewee's subconscious mind to begin collecting information before the interview.

- Schedule enough time for the interview.

- When first talking to the interviewee to make an appointment, avoid launching into a discussion. You will get better information if you schedule the interview, because this allows the interviewee time to think about the topic.

- Plan what questions you will ask, and anticipate what your interviewee might say. Prepare your questions in such a way that you can rapidly take notes.

- Arrive on time.

- Upon arrival, briefly chat informally to establish rapport, but quickly move to the purpose of the interview.

- When starting a conversation, gain permission to take notes and/or to record the conversation.

- Do not attempt to write everything the other person says. If necessary, use a voice recorder to capture the conversation. (Obtain verbal and/or written permission before doing so. If you need written permission, come prepared with a permission form.)

- Minimize noise. Ask the person to turn off music or the TV. When recording a conversation, move away from other sources of noise, such as heaters, air conditioning vents, and open windows.

- Minimize interruptions and distractions. This can take the form of asking the person being interviewed to avoid answering the phone and asking other persons in the office or the home to refrain from coming into the room.

- Ask open-ended questions. Listen patiently for answers. Do not prompt answers.

- Take notes as you listen, even if you record the conversation. When you have questions that need clarification, write them down and ask them later, rather than interrupting the interviewee—let the person talk without disrupting their flow of ideas. Even if answers are lengthy or predictable, do not cut off the person's answers, because you think you know what he or she is going to say.

- As the conversation draws to an end, summarize what the person said and what you learned. If you intend to create a transcript, ask permission to send the material back to the interviewee for his or her review.

- If appropriate, later provide the interviewee with a copy of the corrected transcript, voice recording, and/or notes.

Internet

Once you have exhausted the immediate resources of people close to you, reach out to compiled resources. Today, the internet provides the best source for free and quick information. Google, Bing, and other search engines can identify a wealth of resources. This may be sufficient for your assignment.

For material that was on the internet in the past, but which is no longer online, consult Archive.org. Archive.org also preserves books, audio recordings, videos, images, and software programs. It is a wonderful storehouse of published works.

Wikipedia and its sister projects are powerful resources for getting started. While they are not unbiased, they provide broad understanding on millions of topics. In addition, the Wiki-links and references offer launching points to find more information.

For research by scholars use Google Scholar and Microsoft Academic. In addition, you might want to check into some of the specialized academic databases and search engines listed by Wikipedia at:
en.wikipedia.org/wiki/List_of_academic_databases_and_search_engines.

Government Websites

Government sites also are highly useful. An exhaustive index of US federal agencies is at: www.usa.gov/federal-agencies/.

Wikipedia also provides an extensive index of US government websites organized by branches of the government:
en.wikipedia.org/wiki/List_of_federal_agencies_in_the_United_States.

For economic data, see the World Bank (www.worldbank.org) and the US Federal Reserve Banks (www.federalreserve.gov).

If you cannot quickly find what you need, consider phoning government offices and asking where to locate information. In much of the world, governments are legally required to make information available to the public.

Published Sources

If you believe you need to consult published sources, start with WorldCat (www.worldcat.org). WorldCat is a huge, online catalog of materials from libraries worldwide. It catalogs books, articles, music, and videos from more than 72,000 libraries located in 170 countries and territories. As of 2020, the catalog identified 3 billion items.[6]

If your local library does not have what you need, use an inter-library loan service to access distant sources.

Often it makes sense to purchase books that discuss your topic. Used books generally are inexpensive. Amazon and other booksellers are where to look. Book and product reviews, which Amazon pioneered, are particularly helpful.

Also, consider videos, films, television, radio, podcasts, and audio books for collecting information.

Note Taking

Depending on where you find information, there are different strategies for notetaking.

Printed Materials and Online Text

When you need to read a large volume of material, first skim the documents quickly, consulting tables of content, summaries, and graphics.

When reading the most relevant sources, consider printing the material and then reading it from paper, or read it from a lightweight electronic device. This often results in higher reading speed and better retention. Mark what is relevant and bookmark important sections for later retrieval.

Consider using a text reader for complex materials that you need to understand in detail, such as contracts or abstract concepts. You will find more information on text readers in chapter 7.

Radio, Podcasts, TV, DVDs, and Internet Videos

When watching recorded or streaming media, it helps to have the device controller nearby so you can stop and replay what you are watching. When watching or listening to live TV or radio broadcasts that you will not be able to re-watch or re-listen to, record the program.

When watching internet videos or listening to podcasts, speed up or slow down the playback speed according to the need. YouTube and many podcast apps allow this, but other players do not. A workaround is to download the video or podcast and use Microsoft Windows Media Player to adjust the speed. (You can do this when in the *Now Playing* mode by right clicking on the player, selecting *Enhancements / Play speed settings*, and then using the slider to select the desired speed.)

When listening to or watching something to which you expect to later refer, make a simple outline. Take down people's names and other difficult to remember facts. Also, use a clock or timer to note where information occurs, so you can rewind to that point.

Tools for Capturing Information

Your mind may be sufficient to remember a few simple findings, but as you expand your investigation, you will need tools to capture the abundance of material you will consult. This section discusses these tools.

Paper

Used for centuries—paper with pen or pencil still is the simplest and often the best way to collect information.

Spiral notebooks and 3-ring binders are handy. You also might find 3x5-inch (127x77-mm) cards convenient for notetaking.

Word Processing Software

Most people will use electronic means to capture information both by taking notes and by copying materials. A ready approach is to capture your thoughts with word processing software. If you have many statistics to compile, then turn to spreadsheets.

Microsoft Word's Outline View is excellent for capturing ideas. The Heading Styles feature provides an easy way to create outlines to keep facts organized. You not only can save text, but also pictures and charts by electronically copying and pasting them into word documents. Also, consider using Microsoft Word's Manage Sources feature to capture sources.

Evernote and OneNote

Another approach to notetaking is software designed for making notes, such as Evernote or Microsoft's OneNote.

Conversations and Sounds

Digital voice recorders and smart phones provide the means to capture conversations and make verbal notes. In the past, medical, legal, and law enforcement professionals generally were the only people who could afford to have their notes professionally transcribed. Now, voice-to-text applications are making transcriptions available free to everyone.

Voice-to-Text Applications

Most smart phones, tablet devices, and PCs convert voice into text. The Android and iOS applications are good, if used in a quiet environment, but they generally only function by recognizing a few sentences at one time.

For dictating a lot of material, you will need an application such as Dragon speech recognition, Google Docs Voice, or Microsoft 365 (using the dictate feature). Dragon is $300, Google voice is free, and Microsoft's voice recognition is part of Microsoft Office. These tools work best when the user is in a quiet environment and speaks without pausing. If you learn how to compose quickly, speech-to-text applications can be very productive.

Capturing Graphics

Smart phones, digital cameras, and scanners provide the means to capture graphic materials. Many flatbed scanners are small enough to pack around with a laptop PC, and scanners produce much better scans than the cameras on smart phones.

If you scan text, it is easy to use optical character recognition (OCR) software to convert the scanned documents to text.

Calculations, Drawings, and Sketches

Accountants, architects, engineers, scientists, and other technical professionals often make calculations, drawings, or evaluations using specialized software. Microsoft Excel remains the most commonly used tool for making calculations. Adobe Photoshop, Adobe Illustrator, Affinity Photo, Affinity Designer, AutoCAD, GIMP, Inkscape, and many more drawing programs are available for preparing drawings and editing images.

Scientists often use chemical, mechanical, and electronic instruments. If your documents include calculations, charts, or graphic elements, it is best to complete your analysis and have the results ready as tables and graphics before beginning to write.

Summary

The modern world is exploding with new information and with the means for making this knowledge widely available at a low cost. The writer today possesses tools unthought-of a few decades ago.

Foremost is the internet. In addition to billions of websites and blogs, many of the world's books, printed documents, musical compositions, movies, and videos are now available through the internet. It is likely that within a few years essentially every work ever published or placed into a collection will be available online free or at a modest cost.

However, it still takes a discerning mind to select and organize information to prepare a writing project. The next chapter considers how to make sense of these facts.

Your Personal Plan

What can you do to make your research more efficient?

On your next writing assignment, what can you do to expand your research?

Additional Resources

For videos and more ideas on collecting information for writing projects, go to: www.toweringskills.com/7steps/more/.

Step 3 – Brainstorm

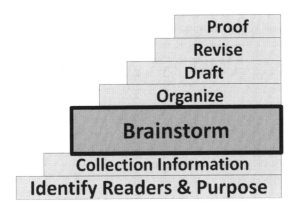

Brainstorming is the technique of quickly and spontaneously creating ideas through imaginative thinking. It is an important prewriting step. It complements the previously discussed activities of identifying your readership, determining your purpose, and doing research. Brainstorming helps link existing pieces of information to your theme and reveals additional insight. This uninhibited thinking helps you mold your thoughts into a full message.

"In writing, there is first a creating stage—a time you look for ideas, you explore, you cast around for what you want to say. Like the first phase of building, this creating stage is full of possibilities." attributed to Ralph Waldo Emerson.[7]

Brainstorming Strategies

You can brainstorm alone or in a group of people. It depends upon the assignment and your circumstances.

Brainstorming works best if it is fast-paced and the participants work without criticizing one another.

Speed

Speed is vital. Set a short time target—say, 5-15 minutes. Work quickly.

Speak whatever comes to your mind. Rapidly capture each idea. Then jump to the next thought. Let the process gallop.

If ideas do not gush forth, keep working until the end of your time limit. Generally, restricting the time and using short bursts of effort will spur creativity. If it does not, consider recycling back to steps 1 and 2 or brainstorm with your sponsor or a colleague.

When done, clarify your notes.

Open-mindedness

Whether working alone or in a group, accept everything that comes. Do not judge. Embrace diverse and unusual thoughts. Let inspiration flow from the complete spectrum of possibilities. Invite novel, crazy, and whimsical notions.

Before you start brainstorming with other people, make it clear to the participants that their contributions will be valued. Establish rules that the participants will not hinder the contributions of others nor judge one another's comments.

Not all ideas will be gems. Nevertheless, capture what might be considered dross as well as precious nuggets. Keep everything—even notions that seem unconnected or inconsequential. Later, you can judge how well the ideas support your thesis. For now, get everything down on paper or captured electronically.

Capture Techniques

Make notetaking as simple and easy as possible.

When working alone, start with a clean computer screen, whiteboard, or sheet of paper. As ideas flow, immediately seize them and summarize them. Write just enough to grasp each thought. Abbreviate.

When working as a group, be fully transparent to the participants. Use a method where everyone can take in what is happening.

Lists

The simplest approach to record a brainstorming session is to make a list of the ideas. Jot down, in a few words, each idea as it pops into your mind or as a participant speaks it.

Note Cards

Another approach to notetaking while brainstorming is to place ideas on note cards, Post-it notes, or scraps of paper. This technique works equally well for small or large groups. It has the advantage of allowing participants to write down their own ideas. Small groups can place their notes on a large sheet of paper, tabletop, easel, or whiteboard, while larger groups can place their notes on meeting room walls or on multiple easel pads.

Mind Maps

Another approach is ***mind-mapping***. Mind-mapping is the creative arrangement of key words on a writing surface. You can use software designed specifically for mind-mapping (discussed below) or write on paper, a dry-erase board, or a chalkboard.

When drawing a mind map by hand, a person working alone or the person serving as scribe for a group places the major idea (theme) in the center of the writing space and then adds key words or short phrases around the theme to depict related ideas. When relationships emerge, the scribe adds lines to connect the associated concepts.

The mapmaker adds words and lines rapidly. He or she arranges them arbitrarily if they occur randomly or places them logically if they are related.

When mind-mapping, do not get hung up organizing the ideas. Rather, capture as many thoughts as practical and with as little effort as possible.

You can find videos and further information on mind-mapping at: www.toweringskills.com/writing/mind-mapping/.

Electronic notetaking is essential if your team is located in different offices and must communicate by phone or other electronic means.

Electronic notetaking also can be handy if later you will share the results with other people.

Many mind-mapping applications enable dispersed groups to jointly construct mind maps and to immediately see their maps grow as participants collaborate. Some of the popular programs for mind-mapping are:

- Ayoa by OpenGenius
- MindManager by Mindjet
- MindMapper by SimTech
- MindView by MatchWare
- Visio by Microsoft

These are just a few of the many products. Although less efficient, collaborators can use drawing, drafting, or presentation software. Further resources on mind-mapping include:

- Wikipedia list of mind-mapping software, en.wikipedia.org/wiki/List_of_mind_mapping_software
- Mind-Mapping.org list of the more than 240 currently operating software products for mind-mapping, www.mind-mapping.org/

So, the choices for mind-mapping abound.

Ishikawa Diagrams

Sometimes a bit of structure helps brainstorming. One of the best approaches is the *fishbone diagram* technique. Kaoru Ishikawa pioneered this method at the Kawasaki shipyards during the 1960s to control quality. He applied cause-and-effect diagrams, which look like fish skeletons, to categorize the causes contributing to problems.

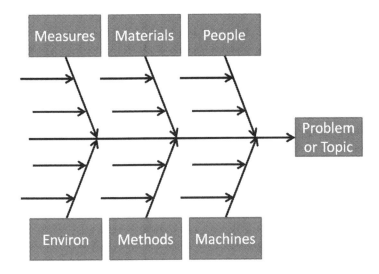

Ishikawa Diagram

Ishikawa used a backbone to represent a major problem, and then added rib bones to represent less important aspects of the problem.

Major categories typically include:

- People
- Machines
- Materials
- Methods (policies, procedures, rules)
- Measures (measurements)
- Environ (location, condition)

An Ishikawa diagram provides a framework for collecting subordinate ideas underneath a primary idea. The categories help stimulate a more complete exploration of possible causes. It is easy for a single person or group to explore each category and broaden their understanding of a topic.

This structured approach generally elicits more ideas. In addition, the technique keeps the ideas organized.

Assess Completeness

After you brainstorm a topic, take a break. Then come back to your brainstorming record. Decide if you collected sufficient material. If you have enough ideas, then move on. If not, repeat the idea generation process or consider using a structured idea-generation technique.

Through brainstorming, you might discover that you need to do more research, redefine your audience, or reframe your theme. Particularly when working on a difficult problem, you may have to cycle back and forth between research, brainstorming, and theme definition.

Summary

Brainstorming is an essential prewriting aide. It improves your ability to discover and link ideas.

Brainstorming has a high benefit-cost ratio. It requires minimal time and yet yields huge benefits.

In the next chapter, you will turn your brainstormed ideas into communication plans.

Your Personal Plan

What can you do to improve your brainstorming skills?

On your next writing assignment, make a mind map or use an Ishikawa diagram.

What will you do to improve the brainstorming skills of your organization?

On your next writing assignment, lead a brainstorming session with at least two other people. Capture the group's ideas with a mind map or an Ishikawa diagram.

Additional Resources

For videos and more ideas on brainstorming, go to: www.toweringskills.com/7steps/more/.

Step 4 – Organize

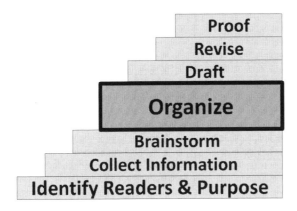

One more thing you need to do before you start writing is to sequence your material. Determine what is most important. Subordinate less important ideas. And then place everything in a logical order, thereby creating a unified stream of thought.

Organization Steps

A good way to start organizing is to:

1. Cluster related ideas

2. Place the clusters in order

3. Add missing elements and eliminate duplicates

4. Strive for unity

Cluster Related Ideas

Working with your mind map, cluster related ideas into groups. If working on paper, a chalkboard, or a dry-erase board, use lines and circles to connect related ideas. When using notes or cards, move the notes or cards into related groups.

Alternatively, transfer your ideas from your mind map to an Ishikawa diagram.

Place in Order

After you have grouped related concepts, determine what is most important and what is less important, and then determine the order that will best appeal to your readers. Decide where your message will start and where it will end, and then select what will follow the start or what will immediately precede the last idea.

Number the major ideas 1, 2, 3, etc., and number the subordinate concepts: 1.1, 1.2, 2.1, 2.2, 2.3, etc. Continue until you have included every concept.

Fill in Holes and Eliminate Duplication

As you proceed, consider what might be missing. Have you answered *who, what, when, where, why, to whom, and how*? Are portions of your message unsupported? If so, fill in those lapses.

Also, look for duplication and eliminate redundancies.

Next, ask yourself if you have the right amount of material. If you have too much, consider what is of minor importance and eliminate it. If you do not have enough, determine what details you should add.

Strive for Unity

Each document should focus on one big idea. Do this by revisiting your plan and determining if the parts contribute to the theme. A well-constructed outline is like a human skeleton—every bone has a purpose, links to another bone, and creates a framework that supports a living human being.

Formal Outlines

Brief documents only need a mind map that you group and sequence, but complex subjects and long documents benefit from formal outlines. Moreover, many technical reports have to follow prescribed guidelines. If this is your case, then move the elements of your mind map or fishbone diagram into an outline that matches the required guideline.

Outline software is indispensable for long and complex documents. Microsoft Word's Outline View is an excellent tool for this. The easiest approach is to use the *Styles* feature to designate heading levels, with the major concepts using the header 1 style and supporting ideas using subordinate levels (header 2, header 3, etc.). You can find more information on Microsoft Styles at: www.toweringskills.com/7steps/styles/.

Google Docs has a similar, but more limited, outline feature.

Templates

Governments, institutions, and trade associations often prescribe document templates. Just a few examples include:

- Securities and exchange commission reports, such as the Form 10-K and Form 10-Q specified by the US Securities and Exchange Commission (SEC)
- Medical, drug, and food reports, such as those prescribed by the US Food & Drug Administration (FDA)
- Environmental reports, such as the environmental assessment (EA) and environmental impact statement (EIS) formats authorized by the US National Environmental Policy Act (NEPA)
- Resource reporting guidelines, such as the National Instrument (NI) 43-101 guideline specified by the Canadian Securities Administrators (CSA) for companies reporting oil, natural gas, and mineral resources

Patterns

If you are not required to follow a prescribed template, consider using one of the following structured approaches.

Development Patterns

Evaluate how your major points support your theme and determine which of the following development patterns best serve your purpose.

- Chronological – good for relating events and telling stories
- Spatial – good for describing geography, real estate, buildings, machines, plants, animals, geology, outer space, or other items where it is important to understand objects in space and how they relate to other objects

- Logical – good for explaining causation and rationale
- Lists – good for providing evidence

With each pattern, consider whether is it better to move from the general to the specific or to move from the specific to the general.

Analyzing Problems

Another useful pattern is the problem/solution model. This consists of:

- State the problem
- Describe the problem
- Identify causes
- Propose solutions
- Justify the best solution

Proposing Change

When proposing change:

- Show the need for change
- State the objectives
- Show steps to achieve the objectives
- Illustrate the superiority of the specified action
- Identify who should take action
- Provide a schedule and a cost estimate for the action

Persuading

When writing about an idea that is hard for your readers to accept:

- Establish your credibility
- Cite your experience, training, and certification
- Say why the new information or behavior change is important
- Tell your readers how they will benefit
- Conclude by asking your readers to take specific action by a definite date

Explaining Complex Topics

When writing on complex topics:

- Introduce and summarize the topic
- Provide an explanation of all important parts or aspects
- Explain how the pieces come together or interact
- Make clear recommendations
- Conclude with a restatement

Sales Copy

A powerful pattern for selling is:

- Gain attention
- Summarize your offer
- Make a promise – describe the benefits of the offer
- Provide proof – cite technical and personal evidence supporting the promise (testimonials)
- Make a call to action – invite the prospect to take advantage of the offer

Copywriters use many variations of this pattern to sell products and services.

Consider Your Audience's Agreement and Interest

If your *audience agrees* with you, present new information to strengthen existing opinions and to maintain interest. If the *audience disagrees* with your ideas, then give both sides of the argument.

If the *audience is not interested* in the argument, place the strongest points first and be brief. On the other hand, when the *audience is interested,* provide more information and place your strongest points last.

Present Testimonials

When providing evidence from people:

- Draw testimonials from those with whom the readers identify
- Consider the effect that the mention of other persons will have on your readers and upon your credibility—some references

will strengthen your standing, while others will undermine your authority

Other Suggestions

Furthermore, do the following:

- Avoid sensational claims and hyperbole
- Use great care when using satire and irony—these techniques are easily misunderstood and can backfire

Capture Attention

Consider how you will capture the readers' attention at the beginning of a document. Here are possible approaches:

- Ask a question
- State a startling or interesting fact
- Share a pithy quotation or aphorism
- Link to a current event, recall a past occasion, or foretell a coming incident
- Tell a short story or relevant analogy

Link the initial part of your message to your readers' interests or needs. Help your readers believe that the document will provide value for them.

Storytelling

An important technique for conveying a message is storytelling. Stories are engaging. They enhance reality and provide a framework on which to hang many details. Readers will remember your stories and the linked facts.

Several non-fiction books that do a great job using stories to teach serious lessons include:

- *Swim with the Sharks Without Being Eaten Alive: Outsell, Outmanage, Outmotivate, and Outnegotiate Your Competition,* by Harvey Mackay, 1988
- *The E-Myth Revisited: Why Most Small Businesses Don't Work and What to Do About It,* by Michael E. Gerber, 1995

- *Leadership and Self-Deception: Getting Out of the Box*, by the Arbinger Institute, 2009

When telling a story, use the following steps:

- Introduce the story by describing the scene. Provide concrete details, but supply them judiciously.
- Introduce the characters. Tell who is involved. Help your readers care about the persons in the story—describe their physical features and interesting facts, and explain motives.
- Introduce a challenge. Draw your readers into the struggle.
- Tell how your characters face their challenges, and show how they triumph over obstacles or are crushed by opposition.
- Throughout your narrative, paint word pictures, but be succinct.
- End the story and make your point. Explicitly—but briefly— emphasize the story's application.

Go light on mystery and suspense. Few people when reading business or other non-fiction documents want heavy mystery and drawn out suspense.

Summaries and Conclusions

Start your document with a summary and end it with a list of conclusions, but compose these sections last. The following chapter will discuss this further.

Persist

As you work through your project, it is normal to feel your ideas are trite or worthless. Many writers experience such doubts.

Roger Angell described, in a forward to the seminal writing guide *The Elements of Style*, how E. B. White—a successful writer for *The New Yorker* magazine—often felt his writing was inadequate and struggled to compose interesting articles. His solution was to persist.[8]

William Stafford offered advice for when you have a low opinion of your work. He said, "Lower your standards, and keep writing."[9]

This is also true of the organizing phase. Keep working. Later sections of this book discuss how to fix any problems if they exist in your first draft. For now, get your thoughts in order as best you can.

Summary

While focusing on your readers and your purpose, sequence your material. Avail yourself of existing development patterns.

Consider using software, such as Microsoft Word's Outline View, to place your material into a formal outline.

Your Personal Plan

What can you do better to organize your ideas before you begin writing?

What development pattern can you use on an upcoming writing assignment?

On a writing assignment, include a brief story.

Use Microsoft Word's Outline View (or a similar tool) to build an outline for a document you plan to write.

Additional Resources

For videos and more ideas on organizing your material, go to: www.toweringskills.com/7steps/more/.

Step 5 – Draft

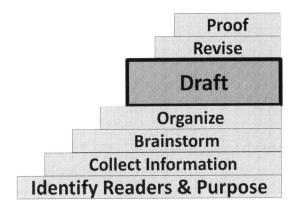

After doing the groundwork laid out in the prior chapters, you are prepared to compose your first draft. The ease of making that first draft depends on this preparation. With little or no preparation, you will find the writing task laborious and protracted. On the other hand, with ample prewriting, you will write faster and with greater ease.

Withhold Judgment

Now, just start writing. And the best way to start is to set aside unrealistic expectations of composing a perfect document in one step, and begin. If doubts arise, say, "I will do what I can. If there are mistakes, I will fix them later."

After you commence, keep going. Using your outline, mind map, or Ishikawa diagram, write at least one sentence for each element. Withhold judgment and move ahead. If you have a message to share—which you came to understand through prewriting—your subconscious mind will have sufficient material to pass to your conscious mind during the drafting step. Often, it seems like magic when the thoughts and words flow.

James Thurber said, "Don't get it right, just get it written."[10]

Find a Place Where You Can Focus

Since drafting requires total concentration, it is essential to work where you will be free from distractions.

Most people work best in a quiet setting. If you are one of these, then minimize noise and commotion.

Some people have conditioned themselves to work well in environments that bustle with activity; but to write, they still divorce themselves from the hubbub by withdrawing into their minds. Malcolm Gladwell is one such person. He states he loves the hustle of a newsroom, and now that he no longer works for a newspaper, he tries to recapture the ruckus by writing in busy coffee shops.

When 32-year old Ray Bradbury drafted *Fahrenheit 451*, he had to escape the pleasant, but distracting attention of his two young daughters. Living on a meager budget, he discovered a basement typing room at the University of California, Los Angeles library. There, surrounded by students busily typing, Bradbury rented a manual typewriter for $0.10 per half hour and drafted his best seller.[11]

In a day when people used quill pen and black ink, Benjamin Franklin wrote in a bathtub. Fortunately, personal computers had not yet been invented, or perhaps he would have electrocuted himself.

E. B. White, author of *Charlotte's Webb* and long-time contributor to *The New Yorker*, secluded himself in a cabin behind his home so he could write.

If you are like most people, find a quiet place, close the door, and ask others to give you a block of uninterrupted time. If you normally work from a desk in the middle of an office with much foot traffic and a lot of noise, then schedule a quiet room, find an isolated desk, or arrange to work from home or a public library. Do whatever it takes to withdraw from the commotion so you can focus and write.

Music

Some people find that listening to music through headphones or ear pods provides the necessary sound buffer from the chatter and clamor of an active office.

Cognitive research has shown that instrumental music from the Baroque Period is particularly effective as background music when focusing on work that requires concentration.[12] Lyrics, thematic music, musical drama, jazz, rock, and rap—although enjoyable to listen to—are more distracting.

Select the Best Time of the Day

Choose a time that is best for you. We all have times of peak performance. Some people write best in the early morning, while others prefer late morning, afternoon, or evening.

Assess your energy levels and the likelihood of interruptions. Find what works.

Take into consideration what activities come before and after your writing time. Many people find their minds are especially clear and creative after physical exercise. If this is true for you, schedule writing time to follow your workout.

Have Your Equipment Ready

Drafting goes best when it moves quickly and with little focus on the recording method. Writers in the past ensured that they had plenty of sharpened pencils, a fountain pen that was in good repair, or a fresh typewriter ribbon. Today methods differ, but you still need to focus on your composition, not on the mode.

Select the method that works best for you. If you touch-type, there is no reason not to compose on a PC. Today, we cannot imagine using a typewriter. If a computer is unavailable, writing by hand is still an option. If you type poorly, writing by hand or using speech-to-text software is a better alternative.

Incidentally, if you do not touch-type, learn. It is an essential skill, which will serve you throughout your life.

In conclusion, before you start writing, make sure your equipment is ready. Do not use a PC or other device that is acting up. Resolve technical problems; then write.

Use Voice Recognition Software

Consider using voice recognition software. It works best if you speak sentences continuously without long pauses and without false starts. Prewriting—having a detailed outline or mind map—can help you rapidly recall your ideas and speak consistently and thus make voice recognition efficient. However, if your thoughts come slowly, then voice recognition probably will not work well for you and could prove distracting.

Although the software no longer needs hours and hours of training to recognize your voice, the technology still requires a quiet place and familiarity with the application.

Microsoft 365, Google Docs Voice, and Dragon speech, are the best voice recognition products available at this time.

For people who write a lot, voice recognition can pay big dividends in saved time.

Go for Speed

As you draft, strive for speed. Type, write, or dictate as fast as you can. Skip mistakes, abbreviate, and add blanks when you struggle for details. Move ahead. Keep your thoughts flowing. Rapidly consult your mind map and outline, and keep writing.

Avoid dredging up details you cannot obtain from your research notes or from brief internet access. If you need to add specific details, which you cannot perfectly recall and which will take time to find, then mark the spot with a blank or ellipse for later addition and move on.

When drafting, stay away from the internet except for quick access to known sources. Going there for other purposes will distract you.

Keep advancing your draft. Get your ideas up on the computer screen or down on paper as swiftly as possible. Later, add facts, figures, and details. If you get stuck when working on one part of a document, move to another subtopic. Add a few blank lines and take up writing on the other part.

Ignore spelling and grammar errors. When using word processing software, some people find it helpful to turn off auto-spelling and grammar checking. The following table summarizes how to turn off these features with the most common word processing software.

Software	Commands to Turn off Auto Spell Check
Microsoft Word	/File /Options /Proofing /Check spelling as you type/
LibreOffice Writer	/Tools /Options /Language Settings /Writing Aids /Check spelling as you type/ and /Check grammar as you type/

If you discipline yourself to keep moving ahead, turning off spell checking and grammar checking may be unnecessary. It is your call.

Another technique to accelerate drafting is to type without looking at what you have written. This is particularly effective with voice recognition software, which tends to confuse homophones and similar sounding words.

In all cases, keep the ideas flowing. Come back later to fix mistakes.

Write Short Sentences

When drafting, try to write short sentences. Later you will find it easier to link overly short sentences, rather than break up long and complex sentences.

Talk to Your Readers

As you draft, focus on your readers. Talk to them as if they were seated in front of you. Conversational writing is easier to read, and writing as if conversing with a person is easier to write.

Control the Tone

Compose in an appropriate tone. Before writing, determine whether your tone should be conversational, direct, colorful, or something else.

An informal, conversational tone includes frequent references to people and ample use of the personal pronouns *you, we, us, I,* and *me.* This tone also embraces the use of contractions, common words, short phrases, and informal grammar.

On the other hand, a formal tone puts people at a distance. It avoids contractions and adheres to more formal grammatical construction.

A direct tone talks straight to the topic. It squares up the facts. It uses simple words, simple sentences, and simple logic.

In contrast, an indirect tone evades direct mention of real issues and meanders circuitously around the outlying margins of the topic.

A colorful tone springs forth with energetic verbs, concrete nouns, and bright adjectives to color and enliven the picture. It embraces metaphors and similes. A lively tone sings and dances.

Meanwhile, a dull tone uses lifeless verbs, abstract nouns, and generic modifiers. Passive voice is common.

Other tones you might adopt include:

- friendly
- intriguing
- sophisticated
- assertive
- gentle
- sentimental
- light
- rational
- expressive
- patient
- earnest
- urgent

In summary, choose a tone that matches your purpose. As you draft, strive to achieve that tone. It is not fatal if you do not achieve a consistent tone at the beginning, but keeping with an appropriate tone while drafting will save later revision time.

Keep a Little in Reserve

Many professional writers say they stop writing before they run out of ideas. They pause mid thought or mid scene, even though they know what they want to write next. They say this helps them resume writing when they return to their work. Hemingway said, "I had learned … never to empty the well of my writing; but always to stop when there was still something there in the deep part of the well, and let it refill at night from the springs that fed it."[13] This technique may benefit you when working on a long project.

Working with Data and Images

Tables, graphs, charts, diagrams, photos, and drawings enhance technical and other informative documents. There are two ways to add these elements to a document. Some people insert them before drafting the text. Others find they can draft most effectively without these inclusions. Use what works best for you and your assignment. However, it is best not to mix drafting with inserting. Do one first, and then do the other.

Draft the Summary and Conclusions Last

Most documents, even emails, benefit from a short summary placed at the beginning of a document and a clear restatement of key points at the end as a concluding section. Write these segments after you have written everything else. If ideas come to you for the summary and conclusion while working on the body of the document, build a list of these thoughts and then later use the list to compose the summary and conclusions.

You also might need to add a list of recommendations or action items to your document. Both the summary and the conclusion sections typically state the recommendations, often in an abbreviated form. The action items can be part of the recommendation or a separate following section.

Consider using numbered lists if you have more than a few conclusions, recommendations, or action items. Numbering them makes them more memorable and provides readers an easy way to reference specific items.

Summary

Draft quickly and uncritically. If you prepared well, the draft will progress rapidly. Hold your corrections until later. Get as much down as fast as you can.

As you become more skilled as a writer, seek to create a consistent tone when drafting.

Insert tables and figures either before or after drafting your text, but not while drafting.

Your Personal Plan

What can you do to draft more effectively?

On your next five drafting exercises, set a time limit. In each instance, the duration will depend upon the length of the piece you are composing and your writing skill. If the piece is short, then set a 10-minute limit. If the piece is long, then increase the time limit to 20-30 minutes. Use a timer. Write as fast as possible for the allotted time. Stop when the timer chimes. Count the words. Compare the word count or the words per minute over the five drafting sessions. Did you improve in speed? How did this affect the quality of what you wrote?

On your next writing assignment, consider what tone best suits your purpose. Strive to maintain the tone throughout your draft.

Additional Resources

For videos and more ideas on drafting, go to: www.toweringskills.com/7steps/more/.

Step 6 – Revise

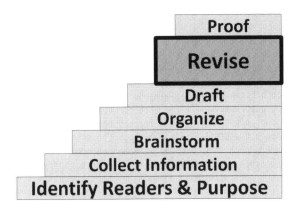

Do you remember being puzzled by a set of confusing instructions? Or, can you recall being bewildered by the fine print of an overly complex legal contract?

If you do, you are not alone. Everyone struggles with complex and poorly written documents.

Contrast those confused thoughts with the clarity you felt when captivated by an article that captured your attention and provided a clear, compelling message.

What made the difference? Why are some documents easy to read, while others are impenetrable?

The answer is sound logic and well-crafted sentences. They are what provide high readability. This is the focus of this chapter—to provide techniques to add clarity and life to your writing. No matter how effective an initial draft is, there are opportunities to be more cogent, concise, and expressive.

Take a Structured Approach to Editing

Editing—the processing of checking, correcting, and rewriting—is a necessary part of all but the simplest writing tasks. This is how we ensure that we communicate effectively. Also, it is how we come to understand our message.

Ernest Hemingway said he threw away 91 pages for every page he published. Leo Tolstoy rewrote Anna Karenina 17 times. So do not despair if you have to revise and revise again to get something acceptable.

Revising is the most time consuming and the most technically challenging aspect of writing. This is the point where you will do the "heaviest lifting." Factors that contribute to the challenge include:

- Ineffective prewriting (steps 1-4)
- Overly laborious drafts (step 5)
- Needing to rethink ideas
- Not understanding effective sentence design
- Having forgotten the elements of grammar
- Impatience—the desire to be done with it
- A lack of editing experience

There are very few circumstances when writing does not need correcting. Even simple emails, text messages, or handwritten notes bear rereading by the author to ensure that words are not left out.

Editing should start with correcting the most serious problems first and then move on to fixing smaller glitches. Here is an ordered strategy, with questions to ask yourself:

1. Serving readers
   1.1. Did I address my readers' needs?
   1.2. Is the tone correct?
2. Quality of ideas
   2.1. Is my thesis clear?

2.2. Is the logic sound?

2.3. Did I include everything necessary?

2.4. Can I delete unneeded fluff?

2.5. Are things in the best order?

3. Language

3.1. Do the words flow naturally?

3.2. Is the grammar correct?

3.3. What can I do to achieve better clarity?

3.4. What can I do to economize on words?

Editing Equipment

Before getting into the techniques of editing, here is a word about equipment. If you compose on a computer, you will want to edit there. It is so easy to delete, copy, paste, replace, and rearrange.

When writing on paper you also can make changes by crossing out and inserting words or adding circles and arrows. While this works well for light editing, major rewrites get messy.

Voice recognition, while good for rapid drafting, is unsuitable for revising. It is easier to move through a document and make changes using a keyboard or mouse.

Remember the Reader

The first step to editing is to assess how well you answered your readers' questions and met their needs. Ask yourself:

- Does the document tell my readers what they need to know?

- Will they understand what I wrote?

- Is the document framed from their perspective?

- How will it make them feel?

- Will it motivate them to agree or to take action?

Answering these questions will help you determine if you have provided sufficient information, used sound logic, sequenced your material for best understanding, and created sentences that communicate clearly.

Another way to keep your readers in mind is to use less instances of *I, we, me, us, mine,* and *ours* and recast your thoughts using the words *you, your*, and *yours*. This may seem like a trivial suggestion, but it can make a big difference.

Develop Your Ideas

Next, check the coherence of your ideas. Does your document illustrate clear thinking? Often, the best way to say something will become apparent only after rewriting it several times.

When editing, look for these problems:

- Unclear theme
- Incorrect assumptions
- Lapses in logic
- Irrelevant information
- Inappropriate amount of evidence—both too little and too much

Once you fix those problems, look at each paragraph and ask:

- Does the paragraph address one idea?
- Does the paragraph have a topic sentence?
- Do other sentences support the idea in the topic sentence?
- Do the sentences follow one another in a logical manner?

When providing a lot of information, consider using bullets or numbered lists.

Grammar

In the same way that chefs understand different ingredients and how they contribute to a tasty meal, persons editing their writing need to understand the basic elements of language—words, phrases, and clauses—and how those elements work with one another. Here is a short summary of English grammar.

Parts of Speech

Parts of speech are categories of words grouped by the way they function in language. Modern linguists have many methods for classifying words according to their function. Those methods provide the most comprehensive explanation of how language works, but for our purpose, the eight traditional *parts of speech* for English are sufficient. They include:

- *Noun*: a concrete or abstract entity: a person, animal, place, thing, activity, event, or idea. Examples: *George Washington was the first president of the United States. His horse ran to the barn. Writing is a challenge.*

- *Pronoun*: a substitute for a noun or noun phrase. *Personal pronouns* include: *I, me, my, mine, we, us, our, ours, you, your, yours, he, him, his, she, her, hers, it, its, they, them, their, theirs, thou, thee, thy, thine, ye.* *Demonstrative pronouns* include: *this, these, that, those.* *Relative pronouns* include: *who, whom, whose, what, which, that.* *Interrogative pronouns* include: *who, whom, whose, what, which.* *Reflexive pronouns* include: *myself, ourselves, yourself, yourselves, himself, herself, itself, themselves.* (There are a few other types of pronouns not discussed.)

- *Verb*: a word that conveys action or states being. Examples: *I saw the dog. He ate his dinner. He is tired.*

- *Adjective*: a modifier of a noun or a pronoun. Examples: *John's long sentences are awkward. I prefer short phrases.*

  - Within the category of adjectives is the *article*. An *article* is a word that marks a noun as being definite (*the*) or indefinite (*a, an*). Examples: *the book, a pencil, an allowance.*

- *Adverb*: a modifier of a verb, adjective, or adverb. Examples: *Short sentences flow quickly. Very long sentences force readers to read slower.*

- *Preposition*: a word that establishes relationship. The most common prepositions are: *at, by, for, from, in, of, on, to, with.* Examples: *The team of experts prepared the report for the client by working from morning to dusk.*

- **Conjunction**: a connector. Examples: *and, or, nor, but, yet, so.* Examples: *She picked up a pencil **and** some paper, **but** she forgot what she wanted to write.*

- **Interjection**: an emotional expression, which is independent of words around it. Examples: ***hi, bye, goodbye, cheers, hooray, good day, farewell, oh.***

Phrase

A ***phrase*** is one or more words that work together as a single unit.

A ***prepositional phrase*** is a phrase commencing with a preposition. Examples: *The team **of** *underline* experts* prepared the schedule **for** the client*.

Clause

A ***clause*** is a combination of a ***subject*** and a ***predicate*** phrase, where:

- The ***subject*** is an actor, agent, or attribute carrier. Examples: *John read the email. **Proofreading long reports** is difficult.*

- The ***predicate*** gives information about the subject. The predicate contains a ***verb*** and possibly other elements. Examples of predicates: *Adam **drafted a long report**. Sue **revised the last chapter**.*

Subjects and predicates can be a single word or many words.

Clauses are either ***independent*** or ***dependent***. An ***independent clause*** can stand alone. Example: ***Martha wrote the report***.

A ***dependent*** or ***subordinate clause*** augments an independent clause. Example: *Martha wrote the report **after she investigated the customer's claims**.*

Conjunctions that often indicate subordinate clauses include: *after, although, as, because, before, how, if, since, so, unless, until, when, where, while, why.*

Pronouns that function as subordinate conjunctions are: *who, which, what, that.* When faced with the decision of using the subordinating conjunctions *which* or *that*, use *that* for clauses that are essential to meaning and *which* for clauses that are nonessential. Furthermore, add a comma to set off clauses that are nonessential to understanding the essence of the sentence.

Sentence

A *sentence* is a group of words that expresses a complete thought. Most sentences include at least one independent clause, thus including a subject and a predicate.

A sentence with only one independent clause and no dependent clauses is a *simple sentence*. Example: *John read the email.*

A sentence with two or more independent clauses joined by conjunctions or by punctuation (comma, semicolon, colon, or dash) and free from dependent clauses is a *compound sentence*. Example: *John read the email, and Nathan read the newspaper.*

A sentence with one independent clause and one or more dependent clauses is a *complex sentence*. Example: *Adam is waiting for the report, which Sue is proofing.*

A *compound- complex sentence* (or *complex-compound sentence*) has at least two independent clauses and at least one dependent clause. Example: *Martha wrote the report, after she investigated the customer's claims, but she failed to take into consideration everything that she had learned.*

When a group of words fails to express a complete thought—that is, lacks an independent clause—it is called a *sentence fragment* or incomplete sentence. Sentence fragments occur when:

- A subject, verb, or object is missing
  - Example (missing subject): *Ran to the barn.*
  - Example (missing verb): *George Washington, the first president of the United States.*
  - Example (missing object): *Matthew received.*
- A group of words is nothing more than a preposition phrase
  - Example: *For the cause of liberty.*
- A group of words is nothing more than a dependent clause
  - Example: *When the tide rolls in.*

The old school rule was never create a sentence fragment. In academic settings, the rule still applies. In formal settings, it is best to avoid sentence fragments, but there are occasions when they prove effective. In informal writing, you will see many sentence fragments.

Do not confuse sentence fragments with sentences written in the ***imperative mood***, meaning they are commands or suggestions, such as: *Keep it simple. Use shorter words. Write shorter sentences.*

Even though these sentences lack a subject, they are not sentence fragments. They are commands. As you have already learned, many of the sentences in this book are in the imperative mood.

Another flawed sentence structure is the fusion of two or more independent clauses into one sentence without punctuation or joining words. This is called a ***run-on sentence***. Example: *James wrote Sue typed William phoned.*

One way to transform this run-on sentence into a proper sentence is: *James wrote, Sue typed, and William phoned.* Another approach is: *James wrote, while Sue typed, but William phoned.*

In the example above of a run-on sentence, it is easy to see that something is wrong with the sentence. On the other hand, it is harder to detect run-on sentences when they occur in long and complex sentences, which contain many prepositional phrases and dependent clauses. The same is true of sentence fragments; they occur more often in long, confusing sentences than in short, straight-forward sentences.

The way to avoid both sentence fragments and run-on sentences is to ensure that each sentence possesses at least one independent clause. Consider the following example of a run-on sentence:

> *Stringing many words together in pleasant-sounding passages and providing ample informative facts to your readers does not ensure meaning or readability this is achieved through sound logic and proper sentence construction.*

Here is the sentence corrected by adding the word *rather* to link the two independent clauses with a semicolon preceding and a comma following the word *rather*.

> *Stringing many words together in pleasant-sounding passages and providing ample informative facts to your readers does not ensure meaning or readability; **rather**, this is achieved through sound logic and proper sentence construction.*

You also could correct the run-on sentence by creating two sentences.

Another Language Element

Another form of language important to writing, which is not a traditional part of speech, is the ***appositive***. An appositive is a noun or noun phrase set next to a noun or noun phrase that provides more information. It is set off with a comma or a dash. Example: *We discussed elements of language—**words, phrases, and clauses***.

Further Reading on Language Structure

There is much more to English grammar and linguistic theory, but these basic concepts are sufficient to discuss good writing. If you need more information on English grammar, see the following Wikipedia articles:

- English grammar
- Parts of speech
- Phrase
- Clause
- Clause syntax
- Sentence
- Sentence clause structure
- Noun
- Pronoun
- Verb
- Adjective
- Adverb
- Preposition
- List of prepositions
- Conjunction
- Interjection
- Determiners
- Articles
- Appositive
- Grammatical mood
- Imperative mood

Another good resource is the Khan Academy course on grammar at: www.khanacademy.org/humanities/grammar.

The remainder of this chapter discusses how to improve clarity.

Keep It Simple – Less Can Be More

The simplest approach to writing better is to write simpler. Focus on one idea and develop it with simple logic. Write shorter sentences. Use simpler words.

Father Tom Allender, S.J. said it well, "If you don't keep it awfully simple, it will become simply awful."[14]

Focus on One Idea

As you edit your draft, you may discover that you have mixed several ideas together. This can occur at the document level or at the paragraph level. If the ideas represent a progression, then great; but if you are simultaneously developing several parallel ideas, it is better to divide distinct ideas into different paragraphs, separate sections, or discrete documents.

Use Simpler Words

Short words often work better than long words. Consider the following examples.

Long Words	Short Words
additional	more
anticipate	foresee
authorize	approve
compensate	pay
cooperation	help
currently	now
designate	show
endeavor	try
indicate	show
inform	tell
initial	first
retain	keep
requisition	order

Long Words	Short Words
solicit	ask
telecommunication	call
investigation	test

Richard Lederer shows the power of short words in the following passage:[15]

> When you speak and write, there is no law that says you have to use big words. Short words are as good as long ones, and short, old words—like sun and grass and home—are best of all. A lot of small words, more than you might think, can meet your needs with a strength, grace, and charm that large words do not have.
>
> Big words can make the way dark for those who read what you write and hear what you say. Small words cast their clear light on big things—night and day, love and hate, war and peace, and life and death. Big words at times seem strange to the eye and the ear and the mind and the heart. Small words are the ones we seem to have known from the time we were born, like the hearth fire that warms the home.
>
> Short words are bright like sparks that glow in the night, prompt like the dawn that greets the day, sharp like the blade of a knife, hot like salt tears that scald the cheek, quick like moths that flit from flame to flame, and terse like the dart and sting of a bee.
>
> Here is a sound rule: Use small, old words where you can. If a long word says just what you want to say, do not fear to use it. But know that our tongue is rich in crisp, brisk, swift, short words. Make them the spine and the heart of what you speak and write. Short words are like fast friends. They will not let you down.

This is not to say that you cannot use big words. If you are a geologist, such terms as "depositional environment" and "Paleoproterozoic tectonic subduction zone" convey precise meanings, and they should be used. This is true for all scientific and business disciplines. Technical writing requires precise phrases and long words. Use the words that convey meaning.

On the other hand, avoid needlessly inflating your vocabulary. If you have a choice between a long word and a short word, choose the short word. Your readers will welcome it.

Economize – Omit Needless Words

Single words often can replace entire phrases. Economize by eliminating extra, needless, unnecessary, redundant, nonessential, superfluous, and excessively elongated and wordy expressions. The following examples illustrate a single word replacing a phrase.

Poor: Wordy Phrases	Better: Single Words
at the current point in time	now
at that point in time	then
call your attention to the fact that	note / see
in support of the idea	thus
performed an evaluation of	evaluated
in most of the cases	often
participated in discussions to determine how to	planned
due to the fact that	because
owing to the fact	because
the reason why is that	because
facilitate a change	update
line-of-sight forward-looking view	forecast

Sometimes entire phrases can be eliminated. Consider the following examples, where ***emphasis*** indicates unnecessary words.

	Poor: Unnecessary Phrase
-	The engineers discussed methods ***that can be taken*** to complete the project.
	Better: Phrase Eliminated
+	The engineers discussed methods to complete the project.
+	The engineers discussed how to complete the project.
+	The engineers discussed completing the project.

	Poor: Unnecessary Phrase
-	***The use of*** insulation is necessary to prevent freezing.

	Better: Phrase Eliminated
+	Insulation is necessary to prevent freezing.
+	Insulation prevents freezing.

	Poor: Unnecessary Phrase
-	The transformer will handle *instances of* 50% additional current.
	Better: Phrase Eliminated
+	The transformer will handle 50% additional current.

	Poor: Unnecessary Phrase
-	The circuits can be used in series *to suit circumstances in which more than one is required.*
	Better: Phrase Eliminated
+	The circuits can be used in series.
+	The circuits operate in series.

	Poor: Unnecessary Phrase
-	The warning light indicated *that* a failure *had occurred.*
	Better: Phrase Eliminated
+	The warning light indicated a failure.

In the following examples, *emphasis* indicates unnecessary words. Underlining, double underlining, and dash underlining indicate thoughts that have been re-expressed more efficiently.

	Poor: Unnecessary Words
-	We *continued the teleconference* discussions with corporate vendors to finalize the requisition purchase order closures.
	Better: Sentence Streamlined
+	We talked to vendors to close the orders.

	Poor: Unnecessary Words
-	They decided to defer shipment of the order until the inspector could arrange an on-site inspection *so that the matter could be resolved simultaneously to his being present.*

	Better: Sentence Streamlined
+	They <u>waited</u> until the inspector could be <u>present</u> before shipping the order. [The last phrase is unnecessary and thus was eliminated.]

	Poor: Unnecessary Words
-	The project manager *continued* to *administer* the preliminary *initial engineering development* design *work* in support of the permitting *activities*.
	Better: Sentence Streamlined
+	The project manager supported permitting by supervising preliminary design.

Consider eliminating unnecessary words, such as *really, very, kind-of, sort-of.*

Also, consider replacing perfect verb tenses when simpler verb tenses work as well. There is a slight difference in meaning, but often the distinction is unimportant. ***Perfect tense verbs*** include the helper words *has, have, had*, and *having*. Consider the following examples.

	Perfect Tense
-	I *have been* reviewing the report.
	Simpler: Without Perfect Tense
+	I reviewed the report.
+	I am reviewing the report.

	Perfect Tense
-	I *have been* considering having the company buy another insurance policy.
	Simpler: Without Perfect Tense
+	I considered having the company buy another insurance policy.
+	I want the company to buy another insurance policy.

In summary, avoid bloat by cutting words that fail to carry their weight.

Prefer Short Sentences over Long Sentences

Short sentences often work better than long sentences. Many style guides recommend keeping the average sentence length to no more than 15-20 words. This provides for some sentences being longer and others being shorter. However, you may find even shorter sentences are better.

The problem with long sentences is they require more time and brainpower to process. This slows the reading process and can reduce comprehension.

Consider the following example. The poor passage consists of 1 paragraph, 2 sentences, and 88 words, thus averaging 44 words per sentence. The second example splits the statement into 2 paragraphs and 5 sentences, reduces the word count to 66 words, and drops the average sentence length to 13 words.

	Poor: Long Sentences
-	Following publication of the document, the Draft Environmental Impact Statement (DEIS) and all ancillary technical reports will at that time undergo public review and comment with any significant comments and changes being incorporated into the document or explained as not being included by the government agency in their publication of a Final Environmental Impact Statement (FEIS). Normally, following the publication of the DEIS, the project is substantially defined from a technical, environmental, and socioeconomic perspective, and the project's impacts to land, water, and air resources are fully defined.
	Better: Shorter Sentences
+	Following its publication, the draft Environmental Impact Statement (EIS) and its supporting technical reports will undergo public review. The agency will revise the draft EIS to produce the final EIS. In addition, the agency will explain comments it excluded. Publication of the draft EIS signals that the agency has fully examined the project. By then, the agency has defined impacts to land, water, and air resources.

Sometimes ideas require long paragraphs, long sentences, and long words, but generally short and simpler writing works better. That said, do not be a slave to short sentences. Using a mixture of short and modestly long sentences and moderate and short paragraphs provides variety and improves interest.

Also, sentences that adhere to the same development pattern can become monotonous. While using good judgment, consider variations.

Other Techniques to Eliminate Wordiness

Write to the point. Take care to avoid verb phrases when single-word verbs will do, such as the following.

Wordy: Verb Phrases	Leaner: Single-Word Verbs
continued to work on the project	**worked** on the project
kept taking the patient's temperature	**took** the patient's temperature

Be aware of "*-ation*" and "*-sion*" words, such as: *action, coordination, customization, discussion, finalization, individualization, initiation, justification, materialization, normalization, operation, participation, rationalization, suspension, transformation, winterization,* etc. Replace these nouns with their corresponding verbs. Here are examples.

Nouns ending in *-ation* and *-ion*	Verbs
action	act
coordination	coordinate
creation	create
expectation	expect
indication	indicate
transformation	transform

Here are more examples of word economy.

	Poor: Wordy
-	We continued to oversee coordination of engineering development work by Bechtel on the preliminary engineering design of the waste disposal system in support of the ongoing permitting discussions.

Better: Streamlined	
+	We coordinated Bechtel's engineering of the waste disposal system. This supports permitting.

Poor: Wordy	
-	Roger continued to engage in work to plan the selection of the preferred route for the water pipe line.
Better: Streamlined	
+	Roger planned the water supply route.

Poor: Wordy	
-	I continued discussions via teleconferences with equipment vendors to finalize closures and suspensions of purchase orders.
Better: Streamlined	
+	I worked with vendors to close and suspend purchase orders.

In summary, keep your writing lean.

Provide Facts

In many instances, your readers want to understand lots of details—this is particularly true with law, government, medicine, science, engineering, business, sales, and finance—and it is not enough just to attach a lot of tables and graphs. While tables and charts help organize data, they are no excuse for not explaining in words the data and the relationships they support. Rather, provide evidence and explain what it means.

Be Alert to Commonly Misused Words

Many people confuse words that are pronounced identically or similarly, but have different spellings and meanings. Do not destroy your credibility by confusing words. The Appendix provides a long list of commonly misused words. Almost no one remembers all of these problematic words and their proper spelling, but you should read through the list to be aware of these words so you are prepared to revisit the list when using the words in the future.

Use Concrete Nouns and Strong Verbs

Use *concrete* nouns and strong verbs. Leave abstractions to philosophers.

Abstract words convey general ideas. Often they are ambiguous. Typical abstract nouns include: *ability, activity, basis, case, character, circumstance, concept, condition, connection, course, effect, effort, extent, facility, factor, instance, intent, interest, manner, measure, method, nature, necessity, order, policy, position, possibility, practice, problem, prospect, purpose, quality, question, reason, relationship, responsibility, result, situation, standpoint, substance, system, type, use, utilization, view.* Abstract verbs include words such as *achieve, characterize, change, develop, do, go, happen, manifest, provide, realize, utilize.*

Concrete nouns represent things that can be seen, felt, touched, tasted, smelled, or specifically identified. Action verbs indicate real movement or activity.

Compare the following abstract words to their more concrete counterparts.

Abstract Nouns	Concrete Nouns or Noun Phrases
authority	State Board of Health / Food and Drug Administration / state auditor / controller / office manager
communication	letter / email / phone call / report
conformity	plus or minus 0.01 mm tolerance
concept	plan to sell a new insurance plan
effort	basic engineering / draft proposal / 120 hours worked
idea	written proposal / preliminary diagnosis / architectural sketch / verbal suggestion
interest	job application / phone call seeking information / email inquiry
obligation	performance contract

Abstract Verbs	Action Verbs or Verb Phrases
achieve	produce 50,000 liters per day / install 55% / proof the report / sell ten new policies
conceptualize	calculate output / draft report / draft a sketch on the whiteboard
conform	not exceed tensile strength of 58,000 pounds per square inch (psi)
endeavor	work overtime / recalculate the loads
remain loyal	stay with current supplier

Many abstract nouns also have concrete meanings. For instance, in the phrase "*instrument case*," the word *case* is concrete; whereas, in the phrase "*the case for reconsidering the design*," the word *case* is abstract.

Even concrete nouns and action verbs vary in their degree of concreteness. Consider the following examples, which contrast *general* words to more *specific* words or phrases.

General Nouns	Specific Noun Phrases
activity	drilling / machining / sandblasting / examining sick patients / selling / writing computer code
analysis	soil testing / x-ray / blood sugar test
design	AutoCAD drawing of the floor pipes
facility	crushing plant / product packaging line / vehicle repair shop / operating room
line	stainless steel cold rolling mill
material	soil / heavy gauge structure steel / 4-mm polypropylene / 1-inch conduit
personnel	waiters / clerks / nurses / technicians / managers
professional	electrical engineer / hygienist / proposal writer
work	excavation / compacted backfill / painting / audit accounts payable

General Verbs	Specific Verb Phrases
analyze	weigh the samples / conduct breakage tests / test the resistance
communicate	send a letter or email / telephone / talk face-to-face / read incoming mail
decrease	decline by 10% per year

General Verbs	Specific Verb Phrases
increase	double in three days
measure	survey with laser transit / gauge with micrometer / weigh / take person's temperature
produce	pump 170,000 barrels per month of heavy crude oil / generate 150 MW / write 600 lines of code
simulate	run Aspen HYSYS modeling software

Often, professionals pile abstractions on top of generalizations, yielding almost meaningless gobbledygook. The following examples illustrate the improved economy and clarity achieved by using concrete nouns and action verbs.

	Poor: Abstract Writing
-	The ability to economize is a policy that should be sought after to a large degree.
	Better: Concrete Writing
+	Encourage thrift.

	Poor: Abstract Writing
-	Achieving a high level of attainment of financial performance can be obtained by the successful utilization of a standard collection of operating practices.
	Better: Concrete Writing
+	Operating standards ensure profitability.

	Poor: Abstract Writing
-	The practice of understanding the requirements of the business relative to financial principles is a reassuring trend in the development of situations that lead to success.
	Good: Concrete Writing
+	Profit and loss statements provide the information investors need.

The following sentence by John Dewey illustrates abstraction taken to the extreme:[16]

Consequences that successfully solve the problems set by the conditions which give rise to the need of action supply the basis by means of which acts, originally 'naturally' performed, become the operations of the art of scientific experimentation.

In conclusion, avoid abstractions—use specific language consisting of concrete nouns and action verbs.

Avoid Confusing Pronouns

Eliminate confusing pronouns. Below are examples.

	Poor: Ambiguous Pronouns
-	The woman talked to her coworker about the problem *she* was having with *her* friend, who kept visiting the office seeking *her* help revising *her* resume to apply for a position at *her* former company.
	Better: Clear
+	Jane talked to Terry about Jane's friend Maria, who wanted to apply for a position at Jane's former company and who kept visiting the office seeking Terry's help revising her resume.

	Poor: Ambiguous Pronouns
-	The inspector told the electrician that *he* made a mistake.
	Better: Clear
+	The inspector said, "I made a mistake."
+	The inspector told the electrician, "You made a mistake."
+	The inspector admitted to the electrician that he made a mistake.
+	The inspector accused the electrician of making a mistake.

	Poor: Ambiguous Pronouns
-	The accountant sat at the desk and worked on her laptop PC. *It* was too small.
	Better: Clear
+	The accountant sat at the desk, which was too small, and worked on her laptop PC.
+	The accountant sat at the desk and worked on her laptop PC, which was too small.

Choose the Right Words

Take care to use words that do what you want them to do. Every word has a history—a public history of how it has been used in the language, a history in your profession, and a history with your audience. Use words that accomplish your purpose.

As you tailor words to your readership, avoid tripping up your readers by eliminating the following:

- Words and phrases that suggest bias
- Value laden words
- Jargon
- Ornamental and extravagant words
- Cute words and phrases
- Vulgar, crude, and coarse language
- Overly informal speech, slang, and dialects
- Excessive use of abbreviations and poorly known acronyms
- Archaic and obsolete words
- Poetic expressions
- Foreign words and phrases
- Unorthodox spelling
- Overly technical words (when simpler words will do)

The following sections amplify this list.

Steer Clear of Gender Bias

The following examples illustrate methods of writing in a gender-neutral manner, when it is necessary to describe a non-specific person or to avoid bias.

Poor: Gender Specific	Better: Gender Neutral
The company mailed each employee *his* check.	The company mailed checks to *all* employees.
The employee should contact *her* supervisor. The employee should contact *his* supervisor.	Employees should contact *their* supervisors. / You should contact *your* supervisor. / The employee should contact *his or her* supervisor.

Poor: Gender Specific	Better: Gender Neutral
Each secretary can contact her supervisor.	Contact *your* supervisor.
businessman / businesswoman	professional / manager / executive
chairman	chair
man hours	hours / labor hours / labor /work hours /shifts
manmade	fabricated / manufactured /synthetic / artificial
policeman	officer / police officer
spokesman / spokeswoman	spokesperson / representative
workman	worker

Also, be aware of bias concerning age, race, sexual orientation, and disabilities. Here are examples.

Potentially Biased	Less Biased
handicapped	disabled
culturally deprived / culturally disadvantaged	minority
the aged / old people / senior citizens	persons over 65 years of age
men / women / males / females	persons / people / individuals
beginner / unskilled worker	new employee / recently hired person

There are times when specific reference to gender or race are important, even required. So, do not eliminate precision in your writing, but use respectful terms.

Note that with some publications, it has become popular to use only feminine pronouns. While this is appropriate for material written for women, when writing for both men and women, it is best to use gender-neutral pronouns.

Some authors switch back and forth between masculine and feminine pronouns when the gender is non-specific. This creates needless confusion. Even using the clumsy *he/she* or *his/her* works better, although superior solutions exist, such as changing singular nouns to plural forms and using the pronouns *they*, *them*, and *their*.

Avoid Value Laden Words

Consider a person, who is upset, who rants the following: *"Overnight it became a real problem! Everybody who was anybody was there! It was criminal!"* In this example, even simple words like *real, problem, everybody, anybody,* and *criminal* take on value. Avoid using value-laden words in any form in your writing.

What makes a word value laden is how the word is used. The same word in another context can be fine.

Avoid Jargon

Jargon is a special term defined in terms of a specific activity, group, or profession. Jargon often is appropriate when communicating within a group, but problems arise when special terminology is used with the public. It is fine for a geologist to write the following when communicating with other geologists and mining engineers:

> *The structure includes intrusive and extrusive igneous rocks derived from a common magmatic source. The quartz porphyry is veined with quartz and orthoclase.*

Nevertheless, this passage is ill suited for most other readers.

Avoid Extravagant Words

Some articulations exhibit a superfluity of sesquipedalia. Neglecting to circumvent the plethora will discombobulate even the most ardent bibliophile's cerebral cortex.

Avoid Cute Words and Phrases

In business writing, avoid cute words, such as *mommy, tummy, itsy bitsy, gee whizz.*

Avoid Profane, Crude, Vulgar, Suggestive, and Coarse Language

This will avert needlessly offending readers.

Avoid Overly Informal Writing, Slang, and Dialects

Yous got that?

Avoid Excessive Use of Abbreviations and Poorly Known Acronyms

Here is an example of excess acronyms relating to the US National Environmental Policy Act of 1969 (NEPA):

> *Not all FAs require a full EIS. Some require EAs first. The finding of the EA determines whether an EIS is required. If the EA indicates NSI, then the LA can release a FONSI and carry on with the PA. Otherwise, the agency must conduct an EIS. Some FAs avoid the EA and EIS, if they meet the CATEX.[17]*

Environmentalists and lawyers might understand this, but few others do. So, steer clear of acronyms for general business writing, unless they are widely understood.

Avoid Archaic and Obsolete Words

Verily, thou shouldst harken to this gardyloo.

Avoid Overly Technical Words When Simpler Words Will Do

Do not write *hyperpyrexia*, when *fever* will do, unless you are a physician or pharmacist.

Avoid Poetic Expressions

Poetry and verse surely serve for wonder and grace,
But beware if poetry finds space in the business place.

Avoid Foreign Words and Phrases

Use foreign words in business writing only if they are essential to understanding. If you are writing about a situation in a foreign country, it may be appropriate to use foreign words. However, if you are writing about common ideas, then use common English words. In other words, *no escribas en español* and *n'écris pas en français*.

Avoid Unorthodox Spelling

If you question the spelling of a word, consult a good dictionary (such as Wiktionary) or do a Google or Bing search using the word plus the word *define* or *definition*. You can find more advice in the spelling section in the following chapter, which discusses step 7.

Subordinate Less Important Details

Successful business and technical writing requires communicating a lot of facts. Doctors, lawyers, engineers, scientists, accountants, analysts, and sales people need to convey abundant, detailed information. This section shows how to provide details without overwhelming readers.

In the same way that an artist creates depth perception by painting close objects larger and in greater detail than similar objects that are farther away, good writers emphasize some details more than others. This creation of perspective holds true at the document level and continues down to the sentence level. Creating this hierarchy of sentence elements is call ***subordination**.

Use Clauses to Subordinate Less Important Facts

One method to subordinate less important facts is to place less important ideas in dependent phrases. The following conjunctions often signal subordinate clauses: *after, although, as, because, before, how, if, since, so, unless, until, when, where, while, why.* Pronouns that can function to create subordinate clauses include: *that, what, which, who.* Both conjunctions and subordinating pronouns signal sentence structure, and in this way, they guide the reader.

Here are examples of subordination.

	Poor: No Subordinate Clauses
-	A schedule for the postponed startup of the new equipment is a concern of the members of the board due to the potential to weaken profits by reducing throughput.
	Better: Subordinate Clauses Used
+	A schedule ***that*** postpones startup of the new equipment is a concern of members of the board, ***since*** the reduced throughput will weaken profits.
+	The members of the board are concerned a schedule ***that*** postpones startup of the new equipment will weaken profits, ***because*** this will reduce throughput.

	Poor: No Subordinate Clauses
-	The need at the company for more space caused by steady growth in staff and more computer equipment required a request by management for an addition to the office.
	Better: Subordinate Clauses Used
+	Management requested an office expansion, ***because*** steady staff growth and additional computer equipment had outstripped available space.

Note the large number of prepositions in the sentences that lack subordinate clauses and the fewer number of prepositions in the rewrites that include subordination.

	Poor: No Subordinate Clauses and Many Prepositions
-	A schedule for the postponed startup of the new equipment is a concern of the members of the board due to the potential to weaken profits by reducing throughput.
	Better: Subordinate Clauses Used
+	A schedule ***that*** postpones startup of the new equipment is the board's concern, ***since*** the reduced throughput will weaken profits.

	No Subordinate Clauses and Many Prepositions
-	The need at the company for more space caused by steady growth in the staff and more computer equipment required a request by management for an addition to the office.
	Better: Subordinate Clauses Used
+	Management requested an office expansion, ***because*** steady staff growth and additional computer equipment had outstripped available space.

So, one way to recognize sentences that may need subordinate clauses is to look for prepositions.

The most common prepositions are: *at, by, for, from, in, of, on, to, with.* These nine words are used 90% of the time when a preposition is present. Other single-word prepositions include: *aboard, about, above, across, after, against, along, alongside, amid, among, around, as, aside, astride, atop, before, behind, below, beneath, beside, besides, between, beyond, but, concerning, despite, down, during, except, excluding, failing, following, given, including, inside, into, like, minus, near, next, notwithstanding, off, onto, opposite, out, outside, over, past, per, plus, regarding, round, save, since, than, through, throughout, till, times, toward, towards, under, underneath, unlike, until, up, upon, versus, via, within, without, worth.*

While most prepositions are single words, some prepositions include two or three words. Just a few examples are: *according to, ahead of, because of, close to, due to, as well as, in case of, in front of.* Most multi-word prepositions include one of the common short prepositions *in, of,* and *to.* You can find a longer list at: en.wikipedia.org/wiki/List_of_English_prepositions.

Good writing does not completely eliminate prepositional phrases, but it does keep them to a modest level.

Writing that weighs all ideas equally, and which abounds with prepositions, is called **catalogical** writing; in other words, details are listed like entries in a catalog. On the other hand, writing that subordinates less important sentence elements is called **analytical** writing. In this usage, *analytical* implies an intricate linking of words and ideas, rather than just listing them.

Use Noun Adjuncts to Subordinate Less Important Facts

Another technique for subordination is to transform independent nouns into noun adjuncts. **Noun adjuncts** are nouns that modify other nouns. Here are examples.

Independent Nouns Linked with Prepositions	Nouns Adjuncts
member **of** the board	board member
equipment **for** computing	computer equipment
addition **to** the office	office addition
schedule **for** installation	installation schedule

Although some noun adjuncts offer word economy, this technique should not go to the extreme, such as the following.

Excessive Noun Adjuncts	
-	water supply tank level evaluation
-	hurricane disaster homeowner policy rider

78

	Excessive Noun Adjuncts
-	excavation permit application delay
-	trip motor transformer investigation report summary
-	heart valve operation equipment technician

Use Adjectives to Subordinate Less Important Facts

A third approach to subordinating ideas is to change prepositional phrases into adjectives. Here are examples.

Poor: Prepositional Phrases	Better: Adjectives
the schedule *for* startup *at* a later date	the *late* schedule / the *delayed* schedule / the *late-startup* schedule
concern *of* the board	*board's* concern
a large number *of* shareholders	*many* shareholders
circumstances *of* interest	*interesting* circumstances

In summary, replace prepositional phrases with dependent clauses, noun adjuncts, and adjectives. This can transform flat, categorical writing into analytical text, which your readers will understand better.

Emphasize What Is Important

Good writing uses the following techniques to emphasize what is important:

- Location in a document – what comes first and what comes last naturally receive emphasis – therefore, place what is important at the beginning and/or at the end of documents, sections, paragraphs, lists, and sentences
- Repetition – summarize key concepts in the introduction, discuss them in the document body, illustrate them with tables and figures, and summarize them again in the conclusion
- Allocation of space – provide more words, sentences, or paragraphs to discuss what is most important
- Details – supply more details to important points
- Contrast – cause one idea to standout by including it with a group of contrasting ideas that are similar to one another but different from the idea to be emphasized

- Climatic arrangement – write in such a way to build suspense and introduce the most important idea as a climax
- Capitalization, bolding, italics, underlining, larger font size, different font style, highlighting, and color—use these mechanical elements to draw attention to the important points

In any sentence, the most emphatic positions are the main independent clause, the subject of the independent clause, and the end of the sentence.

Use Active Voice

Voice describes the relationship between a sentence's subject and verb. When the subject acts, the sentence is *active voice*. On the other hand, when the subject receives action, it is *passive voice*. Passive voice generally includes a form of the *to be* verb—*is, are, was, were*—and a past participle. The following examples illustrate passive and active voice.

	Poor: Passive Voice
-	The agency's comments *were being evaluated* by the company.
	Better: Active Voice
+	The company *evaluated* the agency's comments.

	Poor: Passive Voice
-	The time to drill a new well *is estimated* by the manager to take 3 weeks.
	Better: Active Voice
+	The manager *estimates* it will take 3 weeks to drill a new well.

	Poor: Passive Voice
-	It *was reported* that a revised report *was submitted*.
	Better: Active Voice
+	The clinic *reported* it *submitted* a revised report.
+	The clinic *submitted* a revised report.

	Poor: Passive Voice
-	It *was encouraged* to follow the policy of the company.

	Better: Active Voice
+	The company *encouraged* employees to follow policy.
+	Company policy *encouraged* obedience.

	Poor: Passive Voice
-	Critical business information *is stored* in a special file directory.
	Better: Active Voice
+	The department *stores* critical business information in a special file directory.
+	A special file directory *stores* critical business information.

	Poor: Passive Voice
-	The by-pass circuit *was removed* by the electrician.
	Better: Active Voice
+	The electrician *removed* the by-pass circuit.

In addition to the *to be* verb, *get* and *become* can form passive voice, as the following examples illustrate.

	Poor: Passive Voice
-	If the wire should *get* broken, the signal would *become* distorted.
	Better: Active Voice
+	If the wind breaks the wire, the damage will *distort* the signal.
+	A broken wire will *distort* the signal.

	Poor: Passive Voice
-	The syringe was *gotten* rid of by the nurse.
	Better: Active Voice
+	The nurse *disposed* of the syringe.

	Poor: Passive Voice
-	The boy *got* hit.
	Better: Active Voice
+	The ball *hit* the boy.

Some situations require passive voice. For instance, when those performing action are unknown or unnamed, you may need to use passive voice. For example: *"The office was painted last week."*

Another use is to avoid assigning responsibility or sounding critical. For example: *"The keys were lost."* Instead of: *"James lost the keys."*

A third use is to control focus, such as the following example.

	Poor: Active Voice (Focus split between child and mother)
-	What is the name of the *child* whose *mother* **gave birth** to *him* this morning?
	Better: Passive Voice (Focus maintained on child)
+	What is the name of the <u>child</u> who **was born** this morning?

In the prior example, active voice creates a ping-pong focus; that is, the sentence focuses first on the child, then on the mother, then back on the child; while the passive sentence keeps the focus on the child.

Regarding the control of focus, some people have argued that the second of the following two sentences is better when the writer wants to focus on the *cat* by making the *cat* the subject of the sentence:

- *The dog chased the **cat**.* (active voice)
- *The **cat** was chased by the dog.* (passive voice)

However, the argument ignores the option of making *cat* the subject of the sentence and using active voice as illustrated by the following sentence:

- *The **cat** fled from the dog.* (active voice)

Generally speaking, recasting passive voice into active voice cures other problems with poorly drafted sentences. This occurs, because most of the time active voice:

- Improves the flow of ideas
- Provides more information, by identifying the doer of action
- Emphasizes the doer of action, by making it the subject of the independent clause
- Creates more energy
- Improves understanding

Active voice increases comprehension, because the human mind wants to know *who did what*, and active voice immediately makes clear *who did what*. This enables readers to read active voice faster. And faster reading conveys the genuine feeling that the material is clear and easy to read. However, (as shown before) if active voice diverts focus away from what is important or creates a ping-pong focus, then balance the advantages of active voice against its weaknesses.

The important thing is to be aware of voice and use it effectively.

Make Positive Assertions

State what is—do not state what is not. When expressing negative information, you often can find a simple word to replace a combination of words that start with *not* or *without*. This provides economy and enhances reader comprehension. Here are examples.

	Poor: Negative Assertion
-	The technician did *not pay any attention* to the written procedure.
	Better: Positive Assertion
+	The technician *ignored* the written procedure.

	Poor: Negative Assertion
-	The adjuster did *not include* the water damage.
	Better: Positive Assertion
+	The adjustor *excluded* the water damage.

	Poor: Negative Assertion
-	She left the report *without completing* it.
	Better: Positive Assertion
+	She left the report *incomplete*.

	Poor: Negative Assertion
-	The purchasing agent *did not have any confidence* in the supplier.
	Better: Positive Assertion
+	The purchasing agent *distrusted* the supplier.

	Poor: Negative Assertion
-	The error was ***not important***.
	Better: Positive Assertion
+	The error was ***minor***.

In spite of this admonition to avoid negative statements, there still are many instances where negative words (*no, not, neither, nor, never*) work best. For example:

- *We can't go.*
- *There is no excuse.*
- *No one will attend.*
- *The judge did not decide.*
- *It never snows in Singapore.*

Place the Most Important or Complex at the End

Place what is most important at the end of a phrase or sentence, as shown in the following examples.

	Emphasizes "total agreement"
+	The manager reported to the board that the committee was in total agreement.
	Emphasizes "the board"
+	The committee that was in total agreement reported to the board.

	Emphasizes "important questions"
+	The manuscript is a little disorganized, but it answers important questions.
	Emphasizes "disorganized"
+	The manuscript answers important questions, but is a little disorganized.

When elements in a list have equal importance, place the longest or most complex item at the end. For example: *life, liberty, and the pursuit of happiness.*

Proceed from Known to Unknown

Introduce a topic before commenting on it, and reference what is known before discussing what is new or different. This enables readers to absorb ideas, because they slot the new information into their existing web of knowledge. Here is an example of referencing what is known before proceeding to what is new:

> *I know you like green apples, and I believe you also will like the tart taste of these plums.*

One way to progress from what is known to what is new is to:

1. Start with a phrase such as *"As you are aware"*
2. Follow it with what the reader knows
3. Signal the new information with a word such as *therefore, consequently, however, but*
4. Introduce the new or contrasting information

Keep Related Words Together

Keep associated words together. Here are examples.

	Poor: Related Words Separated
-	The corporation proceeded with the ***investment*** to expand the factory to manufacture a key component for ***$150,000,000.***
	Better: Related Words Kept Together
+	The corporation proceeded with the ***$150,000,000 investment*** to expand the factory to manufacture a key component.

	Poor: Related Words Separated
-	The machinist gave ***gaskets*** to the apprentice with ***neoprene lining***.
	Better: Related Words Kept Together
+	The machinist gave ***gaskets with neoprene lining*** to the apprentice.
+	The machinist gave the apprentice ***gaskets with neoprene lining***.

Poor: Related Words Separated	
-	The vendor sold the hydraulic *drive* to the company *without a motor*.
Better: Related Words Kept Together	
+	The vendor sold the hydraulic drive *without a motor* to the company.

Use Parallel Construction to Discuss Similar Ideas

Express similar ideas using similar construction. This helps the reader rapidly absorb your ideas. This is important when listing activities, such as in a report or plan. Here are examples.

Poor: Different Construction	
-	Last week the planner's activities included: • *Working* with Simmons to get pricing for the IP project. • Sue *will check* the fleet cost. • The two light vehicles *have damaged* windshields. • Service *is due* for the grader. • *Reviewed* the invoice from CP Equipment.
Better: Parallel Construction	
+	Last week the planner: • *Worked* with Simmons to get pricing for the IP project. • *Asked* Sue to check the fleet cost. • *Arranged* windshield repairs for two light vehicles. • *Scheduled* service for the grader. • *Reviewed* the invoice from CP Equipment.

Poor: Different Construction: Sentences in one paragraph using differing verb tenses	
-	I *am working* with Simmons to get pricing for the IP project. Sue *will check* the fleet cost. The two light vehicles *have* damaged windshields. Service *is* due for the grader.

	Better: Parallel Construction: Sentences in one paragraph using consistent verb tense
+	I *am working* with Ray to price the IP project. *Sue is checking* the fleet cost. We *are arranging* to repair the two vehicles with damaged windshields. We *are planning* to repair the grader.

Parallel forms also improve individual sentences, as shown by the following examples.

	Poor: Different Construction
-	I am concerned *with his being late*, and *he did not prepare*.
	Better: Parallel Construction
+	I am concerned he was *late* and *unprepared*.

	Poor: Different Construction
-	It was both *a difficult assignment* and *tiring*.
	Better: Parallel Construction
+	The assignment was *difficult* and *tiring*.

	Poor: Different Construction
-	The company's having experienced employees, a project portfolio, which is large, and making a lot of money from investments enabled the company to compete effectively.
	Better: Parallel Construction
+	The company's *experienced employees*, *extensive project portfolio*, *and successful investments* enabled the company to compete effectively.

	Poor: Different Construction
-	Career success comes from being at the right place during times that are good and being recognized as not causing trouble.
	Better: Parallel Construction
+	Career success comes from *being* at the right place at the right time *doing* the right things.

	Poor: Different Construction
-	The project is *under budget*, and it is *taking less time than forecast*.
	Better: Parallel Construction
+	The project is *under budget* and *ahead of schedule*.

Occasionally, you may want to repeat the same preposition or other words in a series to create emphasis. You will not want to over use this device, but here is an example of its use.

	Adequate Parallels
-	The stonemason laid the tile on the wall and floor.
	Stronger Parallels
+	The stonemason laid the tile *on the* wall and *on the* floor.

When multiple sentence elements (phrases and clauses are long), the technique illustrated above can prove useful. For example:

> *To prepare to deliver a presentation, before you speak, relax your body **by** taking several deep breaths, **by** stretching your arms and legs, and **by** slowly moving your head from side to side and nodding up and down to stretch the muscles in your neck.*

In summary, parallel writing improves readability. In fact, parallel writing can make words truly memorable, as demonstrated by these famous quotations:

> *"**Ask** not what your country **can do** for you; **ask** what you **can do** for your country."* — spoken by John F. Kennedy, written by Kennedy in conjunction with his speechwriter Ted Sorensen

> *"... we here highly resolve that these dead shall **not have** died in vain—that this nation, under God, shall **have** a new birth of freedom—and that government of **the people**, by **the people**, for **the people**, shall **not** perish from the earth."* — Abraham Lincoln

Use Different Constructions for Variety and Development

Always using the same words or the same type of sentences can prove monotonous. To improve interest:

- Use synonyms
- Use pronouns
- Structure sentences differently
- Vary sentence and paragraph length

The following example uses synonyms and pronouns to provide variety.

	Use of Synonyms
+	The *crew* began the excavation at 6 AM, with the *team* consisting of *five employees*. *They* commenced *their* work by cutting into the concrete. As this activity progressed, the *workers* brought in a backhoe to scoop out the broken material. The next step involved the *laborers* digging a 5-foot trench paralleling the pipe …

Only your imagination and keeping your sentences within reasonable limits of length and complexity should limit your innovation. Rather than using many short sentences, consider forming some longer sentences that subordinate less important details as dependent clauses and/or phrases. Here are examples.

	Short Monotonous Sentences
-	I was concerned. He was late. He did not prepare. It made a difficult assignment more complex. This consumed precious time.
	Longer Sentences Subordinating Ideas
+	I was concerned that he was late and unprepared, because this made a difficult assignment more complex, thus consuming precious time.

	Short Monotonous Sentences
-	The company employs many experienced people. The project portfolio is large. Various investments make a lot of money. The company competes effectively.

	Longer Sentences Subordinating Ideas
+	The company competes effectively, because it has many experienced people and possesses a large portfolio of profitable investments.

As already stated, from time to time, you will want to construct different sentence structures. Most sentences follow one of the following patterns (or any combination of the patterns, if the sentence is a compound sentence).

Subject	Verb

Subject	Verb	Object

Subject	Verb	Complement

Here are examples that illustrate alternative patterns. However, be careful to keep your sentences sounding natural.

	**Subject	Verb**
+	A boulder lay by the road.
	**Verb	Subject**
+	By the road, lay a boulder.

	**Subject	Verb**
+	The company prospered.
	**Verb	Subject**
+	Thus, prospered the company.

	**Subject	Verb	Object**
+	I investigated his performance.
	**Object	Subject	Verb**
+	His performance I investigated.

You also can introduce variety by beginning sentences with:

- Adverbs – example: ***Suddenly***, *the mill exploded.*

- Adverb clauses – example: ***Although the account was closed,*** *the firm still refunded my money.*

- Prepositional phrases – example: ***At the close of the market,*** *the company stock reached a new high.*

- Participial phrases – example: ***Anticipating a slow buildup of pressure****, the control room operator placed the reactor on standby.*

- Conjunctions – example: *We discussed all the comments made on the prior report, resolved concerns, and obtained agreement.* ***But,*** *we did not make an action plan.*

- Appositives – example: ***A unique approach****, whistle-stop promotions achieved much media attention.*

In conclusion, add variety. Just do not get so cute that you create confusion or lose credibility.

Check the Sound

For writing to be intelligible, it should sound natural. The best way to test for unaffected flow and clarity is to hear your words. You can do this by reading it aloud, by asking someone else to read it aloud, or by using software to read it aloud.

Text Readers

Text-to-speech readers are powerful tools for improving your writing. Good text readers include:

- Microsoft Office's built-in reader called Speak in older versions and Read Aloud in newer versions

- Natural Reader by NaturalSoft Ltd., www.naturalreaders.com, $100-$200

- Balabolka by Cross+A, www.cross-plus-a.com/balabolka.htm, free

Most smart phones and many electronic tablets also have built-in text reading capability.

Use Transitions

When checking the sound of your writing, look for transition words and phrases connecting sentences and paragraphs. If they are missing, add them. Transitions signal the directional flow of ideas. They clue readers to:

- Arrangement – *above, below, beside, in front of, ahead of, after, behind, following, ...*

- Timing – *before, after, at the time of, simultaneously, weeks before, months after, ...*

- Logical relationships – *consequently, however, notwithstanding, since, therefore, thus, ...*

Fix Capitalization and Punctuation

Correcting capitalization and punctuation are part of both the editing and the proofing processes. For the sake of simplicity, the next chapter discusses capitalization and punctuation.

Attend to Page Layout and Design

In addition to the topics discussed, give attention to the document's page layout and design. That is, check:

- Titles and headings
- Page size, page layout, and page numbering
- Columns and margins
- Quotations
- References, footnotes, and endnotes
- Positioning, naming, numbering, and formatting of tables, charts, graphs, photographs, diagrams, and text boxes
- Bullet and numbered list styles
- Font selection, font size, kerning (the horizontal space between letters), vertical line spacing, and fonts for emphasis and strength

A big part of succeeding with document page layout is being consistent. It helps to develop or borrow a standard and follow it. These standards are called ***style guides***.

The other essential ingredient to getting the design correct is investing the time to check and fix all the small details. This takes patience and diligence. Yes, it is work. But, it is work that pays dividends, because a well-written document, free of errors, and consistently formatted shows respect for your readers. Furthermore, it fosters their reciprocal esteem for the author and for the institution that the author represents.

Practice

Practice is indispensable to learning how to edit. You learn by doing. Start with where you are now and determine that you will improve at least one aspect of your writing. Perhaps it is to write shorter, simpler sentences. Maybe it is to use more active voice. Perchance it is to subjugate ideas. Whatever it is, get started and go from one technique to the next. In time, the techniques will become second nature. And, gradually—but ever so surely—your skill as a writer will grow.

Summary

Keep your readers in mind as you edit. Keep asking, "Will they understand this?"

Keep sentences and paragraphs short and effective.

Use short words, but do not slavishly avoid long words and technical language if they provide precision and clarity.

Subordinate less important information.

Strive to eliminate passive voice.

Make positive assertions.

Use parallel construction when presenting similar ideas.

Eliminate confusing pronouns, emotional expressions, bias, and misused words.

Keep related words together.

Practice. The more you write and rewrite, the stronger your skills will become.

Your Personal Plan

What will you do to simplify your writing?

What are the three most important editing principles that can improve your writing?

On your next writing assignment, apply two of the techniques from this chapter to improve your document. Do this by making two passes through the document, with each pass focusing on one principle.

Additional Resources

For videos and more information on revising, go to: www.toweringskills.com/7steps/more/.

Step 7 – Proof

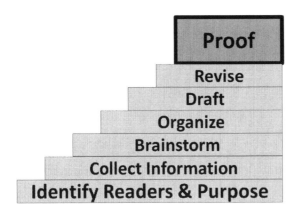

Have you ever spent a lot of time proofing a report, thought it was finally done, and sent it out, only to learn later that it contained stupid and embarrassing errors?

Even simple errors can make you look bad. Mistakes of any type diminish your credibility. Writing errors are similar to carrots covered with dirt from the garden—the carrots are nutritious, but no one is willing to eat them until the dirt has been washed off. In a similar way, when you fail to correct annoying errors, you are going to turn off readers.

An old saying goes, "Check everything twice." This is especially true when proofing an important document. In fact, twice might be only half enough.

Determine the Right Amount of Proofing

A document's purpose helps determine the appropriate amount of proofing. Something you write for yourself may need little if any proofing, but documents intended for others require some rechecking. Even a short text message you prepare on your phone can benefit from a quick reread before you press "send." Meanwhile, long, complex, business documents require thorough and systematic proofing, especially if the audience is fussy.

Give Yourself Time

If possible, let your document set for at least 30 minutes—overnight is even better. Setting your writing aside will clear your mind and help you view your document with a fresh perspective when you return to it. You will find more errors and see better ways of saying things. Consequently, you will produce a better product.

When budgeting time to produce a long document, schedule adequate time for thorough proofing.

Take a Sequenced Approach

With many aspects to consider, it helps to proof systematically. Sweat over the big things first. Then move to smaller details. Do not waste time carefully proofing spelling and fine tuning punctuation if whole sections of the report are redundant or awkwardly phrased. Do major deletions and heavy rewriting before fine-tuning.

This does not mean that you cannot correct an error as you see it, but you should make multiple passes through a document looking for fundamental errors first. Consider using this punch list for making corrections:

1. Substance
2. Logic
3. Organization
4. Transitions
5. Word choice
6. Grammar
7. Spelling

8.   Capitalization
9.   Punctuation
10. Overall visual appearance

Substance

Does the piece provide readers what they need? Do you address all the important issues? Do you provide sufficient details? Will your message evoke the response you desire?

Logic

Is the logic sound? What can you do to make the reasoning easier for your readers to follow?

Organization

Is the document well organized? Do the parts fit together to build a whole message? Do the elements follow one another in the best sequence?

Transitions

Do your ideas flow naturally? Did you use transitional phrases and words to link sentences and paragraphs?

Word Choice

Do your words create the right tone? Are your words clear, precise, and vivid?

Grammar

Is the grammar correct?

Spelling

Are the words spelled correctly?

Capitalization

Does capitalization adhere to common practice or to your style guide?

Punctuation

Is the punctuation appropriate?

Visual Appearance

Is the document aesthetically appealing? Are the headers, footers, titles, and section headings attractive and consistent? Are figures and tables clear? Are line spaces and margins consistent? Does the document balance white space, text, and images?

Read Aloud

At some point in the correction process, you should read the document aloud. Nothing helps more to identify problems in logic, flow, and word choice than vocalizing or hearing the text.

Even better than yourself reading aloud the document, is using text-to-voice software to hear the text. This not only helps you evaluate your logic and flow, but it also helps immensely to spot wrong words or words left out.

Print or Reformat the Document

Some people find it helpful to print a document and read it from paper. Another approach is to temporarily reformat the document in a different font or change the number of columns and then proof it.

Get Help

When possible, enlist a family member, friend, or colleague to read the document with an eye for content. Ask them to point out unclear ideas, lapses in logic, and awkward phrases. Later, ask another person—one with a skill for finding small errors—to proof the document for spelling and punctuation.

If you are a non-native speaker of English, obtain the help of a native English speaker. If time allows, work together with one person reading the document aloud and the other looking at the printed text.

If you do not have access to a native English speaker, use translation software to pass the text back and forth between English and your native language. Draft in English. Then use software to translate your English draft into your native language. See how it reads. Correct the document in your native language. Then use the software to translate your document back into English and compare the retranslation with your original English composition. This can help you spot nuances that you missed in your draft. This is an imperfect process, but it can prove helpful when you do not have access to a person fluent in both languages.

If you want to improve your ear for English, establish a practice of daily oral reading. This, coupled with listening to electronic media, will help train your mind to create natural sounding English prose.

Track Changes

When working with other people, it helps to use a redlining feature to keep track of changes. To use Microsoft Word's tool, go to */Review /Track Changes/*. You can show revisions in-line or as balloons at the side of the document.

Use Spelling, Grammar, and Style Checking Software

The software products for checking spelling, grammar, and writing style are indispensable tools. They cannot catch all errors, but these apps recognize many problems and offer many good suggestions.

Microsoft Word

The grammar and style checker built into Microsoft Word is excellent. You activate grammar checking with the F7 key or the command: */Review /Spelling & Grammar/*. To gain access to its full power, execute the command: */File /Options /Proofing /When correcting spelling and grammar in Word/*, then turn on the following features:

- Check spelling as you type
- Use contextual spelling
- Mark grammar errors as you type
- Check grammar with spelling
- Show readability statistics

In the */Writing Style/* selection box, you can select either:

- Grammar Only
- Grammar & Style

You will obtain the most help if you select **Grammar & Style**.

From the */Settings/* link, you can customize your experience choosing from a large number of grammar and style options. Microsoft Word defaults with the style options turned off. I recommend turning the style option on so you can have more tools to critique your writing.

Readability Indexes

If you select */Show readability statistics/* as an option, Microsoft Word will generate word counts and scores for:

- Portion of sentences using passive voice
- Flesch Reading Ease
- Flesch-Kincaid Grade Level

As discussed in the prior chapter, passive voice generally is harder for readers to understand.

Rudolf Flesch (1911-1986) developed the **Flesch Reading Ease** evaluation; and he and J. Peter Kincaid (1942-) created the **Flesch-Kincaid Grade Level** index. Both systems use word length and sentence length to measure the difficulty of understanding text. Shorter sentences and shorter words increase the Reading Ease score, but decrease the Grade Level score.

The maximum Flesch Reading Ease score is 120. Young readers readily understand scores of 80 to 100, while very mature readers only understand scores of 0 to 30. Thus, higher scores are better, because they represent easier to read text.

On the other hand, the Flesch-Kincaid Grade Level scale goes in the other direction: lower scores are better. Flesch-Kincaid Grade Levels match US school grades 1 to 12. With very short sentences and monosyllabic words, it is possible to obtain Flesch-Kincaid Grade Level scores below zero, while scores above 12 are possible with very long sentences and long words.

Readability statistics are very useful. You will improve your writing by keeping the Flesch-Kincaid Grade Level and the passive voice score low.

Other Grammar-Checking Software

If you feel you need additional help with grammar and style checking, consider one of the many stand-alone grammar-checking programs. Some are free, while others are quite expensive.

While grammar-checking programs are helpful, they do not replace an understanding of grammar, vocabulary, and effective writing styles. Blindly following the advice of grammar checkers—even the best—can still lead to foolish mistakes. So, use them, but keep alert to problems they fail to spot.

Obtain More Spelling Help

English spelling is difficult, because the language absorbed many words from many other languages, experienced numerous changes in pronunciation, and now uses different ways of spelling.

Internet Search Suggestions

When challenged by a difficult to spell word, use an internet search engine. By default, Google, Bing, and Yahoo provide hints and auto-completion. Just start typing a few of the letters in the search box and often you will find the illusive spelling. (If your Google page fails to show suggestions, sign in and change the preferences at: www.google.com/preferences.)

Also, if you question the spelling of a word, perform a search with the word in question accompanied by adjacent words from your composition or by words of similar meaning. Generally, the browser will suggest the correct spelling, and the search results will verify if the word means what you think it does. This can distinguish words that are confusing, such as *bare* and *bear*.

Online Dictionaries

Other tools are online dictionaries. The easiest to use are those built into Google and Bing. Just type the word in question preceded or followed by the word *define* or *definition*. These integrated dictionaries are far better than most other online dictionaries, because they are free from distracting advertising.

If you need a more detailed dictionary use Wiktionary. It is thorough, fast loading, and free of advertising.

Watch Out for Words People Confuse

Spell-checking software usually cannot detect words spelled correctly, but used inappropriately. Such mistakes must be recognized by a human being who thoroughly understands the language and reads every word. You need to be aware of words that often get confused and watch for their presence. This book's Appendix explains most of these troubling words. If you will familiarize yourself with the list, you will be better prepared to detect them and avoid misusing them.

Capitalization

Typically, you will use capital letters for:

- The first word of sentences and quoted sentences.

- Proper nouns, which include names for specific persons, organizations, and places.

- Abbreviations of words that are capitalized, such as *US, UK, EPA, IRS, GM, Mr., Mrs., Ms.*, but not abbreviations of words that normally are not capitalized, such as *ft* (feet), *mm* (millimeters), *mph* (miles per hour), *e.g.* (exempli gratia, for example).

- The pronoun *I* and all contractions that contain it, such as *I'm* and *I'll.*

- Creative works: books, short stories, poems, plays, songs, record albums, movies, CDs, DVDs, art works, non-common games, and courses of instruction. Only capitalize articles (*a, an, the*), conjunctions (*and, or, but*), and short prepositions if they are the first word of a title, such as *A Man for All Seasons* or *The Good Earth.*

- Important events and eras, such as *Christmas, Early Medieval Period, Paleozoic Era.*

- The words *President* and *Prime Minister* when referring to a specific chief government leader.

- Titles that precede proper names, such as *Congresswoman Pelosi, Senator Goldwater, General Grant.*

There is no need to capitalize professional titles. For example: *vice-president, general manager, sales representative.*

Some style guides and editorial policies call for capitalizing all names, pronouns, and synonyms for God, such as *Master, Savior, Redeemer,* etc. This convention was nearly universal in the 19th Century and early 20th Century, but the current trend is to use less capitalization for pronouns and synonyms of deity.

Capitalize only those words that truly need capitalization. There is a tendency in American business to capitalize more words than necessary. Generally, this reduces reading speed, and that reduced reading speed signals to the brain that the material is more difficult to comprehend. Therefore, to keep your readers reading quickly, minimize capitalized words, while still capitalizing the words that require it.

Science and engineering have standards for capitalizing scientific and engineering units. The most common standard is the International System of Units (SI). A description is at: en.wikipedia.org/wiki/International_System_of_Units.

The *US Government Printing Office Style Manual* (www.govinfo.gov/app/details/GPO-STYLEMANUAL-2016) is another useful guide to capitalization.

Last of all, AVOID ALL CAPITALS, even for document titles or headings. Using all capitals dramatically slows reading and suggests the writer is **SHOUTING**.

Punctuation

This section summarizes the best practice for punctuation.

A *period* (.) indicates the end of a sentence or the end of many (but not all) abbreviations. In all English speaking countries, except the US and Canada, the period is called a *full stop*.

During the approximately 100 years when much written material was prepared on typewriters with uniform type width, the best practice to end a sentence was to place two character spaces after the period, question mark, or exclamation mark that ended a sentence. This helped readers spot the end of sentences. When typewriters gave way to word processors and variable-width fonts, the practice of using two spaces at the end of sentences declined.

Then, during the 1990s, the developers of Hypertext Markup Language (html), which is the code use by the World Wide Web, configured the code to ignore extra spaces. To show more than a single character space on a webpage, a person needs to add special characters (such as the non-break space) or use other html code. This was extra work, and consequently, most web content stopped using double character spaces at the end of sentences.

This is how html continues to behave. So now, most people use only one space at the end of a sentence.

In spite of this shift to a single space, evidence shows that using two spaces at the end of each sentence is better. Clinical tests reveal that the added space improves reading ease for nearly all readers and increases reading speed for some people.[18] This is why this book is typeset with two spaces after each period. Every little thing you can do to improve your readers' experience is worth the effort.

With email, Microsoft Word, Google Docs, and other word processors, it is still possible to display multiple character spaces just by typing the space key multiple times.

Periods often appear at the end of abbreviations, such as *Mr.*, *Mrs.*, *Ms.*, *etc.* and the use of initial letters for proper names, such as *J. K. Rowling*. Some style guides use periods for abbreviations, such as *U.S.*, *U.K.*, and *E.U.*, while others dispense with periods, such as *US*, *UK*, and *EU*.

Commas (,) separate items in lists, set off clauses, and set off words that interrupt flow. Much more could be said about how to use commas, but this is enough to get started. Consult Wikipedia or a style guide for the intricacies of comma use.

A **semicolon** (;) joins two independent clauses, when a conjunction is absent; this sentence is an example of this use. In addition, you can use semicolons to separate items in lists, especially when the elements each contain commas; in this instance, semicolons become "super-commas."

Some people dislike semicolons, finding them too formal; however, there are occasions when nothing works better than a semicolon to connect two independent clauses when the ideas are closely related. A dash can serve the same purpose, and it has a modern feel. Be aware of prejudices and regulate your use of semicolons and dashes according to your readers' preferences.

A *colon* (:) starts a list, sets off information, or separates numbers used in groups, such as:

- Ratios. Example: *3:1*, meaning the ratio of three to one
- Time. Examples: *3:35 PM* and *17:23:00 UTC*
- Book citations. Examples: *Genesis 1:27*, indicating chapter 1 and verse 27; *Encyclopædia Britannica (11ᵗʰ edition) 9:587*, indicating volume 9, page 587

A colon also can join two independent clauses when the second clause repeats or expands the idea from the first clause. Example: *She went to town: she rode her bicycle into the village.*

Book titles often use colons to separate the main title from the subtitle. Example: *Blink: The Power of Thinking Without Thinking.*

Some style guides use a colon to separate locations from publishers when providing publisher information in bibliographies, footnotes, and endnotes. Example: *Oxford, UK: Oxford University Press.*

A *hyphen* (-) joins two words used as one. Instances of its use include:

- Words used as a single adjective. Examples: ***one-trick*** *pony,* ***black-eyed*** *Susans,* ***multi-functional*** *feature*
- Number followed by a unit of measure when used as an adjective. Examples: ***5-ton*** *truck,* ***12-pound*** *hammer*
- Compound numbers. Examples: ***twenty-one,*** ***fifty-seven*** *thousand*
- Potentially confusing prefixes and suffixes. Examples: *John* ***re-covered*** *the leaky roof. The organization is* ***semi-independent.***
- Span of numbers or letters. Examples: ***1939-1945, A-Z***

Dashes (– and —) set off words or phrases—they add emphasis or provide more information. Commas or semicolons serve the same purpose, but dashes provide greater clarity, especially if a sentence already has commas. The two types of dashes are:

- *Short dash*, called *en dash* (–), which:
  - Indicates an abrupt change in thought – like this
  - Sets off an appositive
  - Marks a span, such as *1939–1945*
- *Long dash*, called *em dash* (—), which:
  - Indicates an abrupt change in thought—like this
  - Sets off an appositive
  - Sets off the source of a quotation

Standard keyboards do not have dashes. To add them to documents, do one of the following:

- Select the short or long dash from a list of special characters or symbols (for example, in Microsoft Word they are found at: */Insert/ Symbols/ More Symbols/ Special Characters/*)
- Generate a dash by using a computer numeric keypad to enter one of the following numbers while holding down the Alt key:
  - **0150** to obtain a short dash
  - **0151** to obtain a long dash
- When using Microsoft Word:
  - Obtain a short dash by typing a word, a space, one or two hyphens, a space, another word, and a space
  - Obtain a long dash by typing a word, two hyphens, another word, and a space

Sometimes you will see two (or even three) hyphens used to indicate a dash when the dash symbol is unavailable.

While short and long dashes both set off an appositive or signal an abrupt change, be consistent throughout a document.

For more information on dashes see: en.wikipedia.org/wiki/Dash.

Parentheses (()) set off additional information, which is secondary in importance.

A *question mark* (?) ends a question.

An ***exclamation mark*** (!) indicates strong feeling. Technical and business writing should use exclamation marks seldom, if ever.

An ***ellipsis*** (…) shows the omission of words. Much informal writing on the internet and some sales material overuses or incorrectly uses ellipses to try to provide emphasis, continuity, or informality. Use this punctuation mark sparingly; otherwise, you will reduce your credibility.

An ***apostrophe*** (') marks the omission of letters to form a contraction, and it indicates a possessive form of a noun. Examples of contractions: *can't, don't, I'll, they'll.* Examples of possessives: *Martha's, Samuel's, Congress's, dog's, dogs'.*

Many older style manuals recommend adding only an apostrophe (without the letter *s*) after words that already end in the letter *s* (such as *James', Charles', Augustus'*), but this practice is giving way to a more consistent use of the characters *'s* after all words ending in the letter *s* (as in *James's, Charles's, Augustus's*).

The possessive form of the word *it*, which is *its*, drops the apostrophe so as not to be confused with the contraction of *it is*, which is rendered *it's*.

For more information on apostrophe see:

- en.wikipedia.org/wiki/Apostrophe
- en.wikipedia.org/wiki/English_possessive

Quotation marks (" " and ' ') indicate quoted material or emphasized words. In many settings, overuse of quotation marks for emphasis also reduces your "credibility."

The following table summarizes punctuation norms.

	Mark	Use
.	Period	Ends a sentence. Ends some abbreviations.
,	Comma	Separates items in lists. Sets off clauses. Sets off words that interrupt flow.
;	Semicolon	Joins two independent clauses. Separates items in lists when elements contain one or more commas.

	Mark	Use
:	Colon	Starts a list. Sets off numbers. Joins two independent clauses when the 2nd clause repeats or expands the idea from the 1st clause.
-	Hyphen	Joins two words used as one word. Joins a number to a unit when used as an adjective.
—	Dash	Sets off and emphasizes words or phrases.
( )	Parenthesis	Sets off and de-emphasizes words or phrases.
?	Question Mark	Ends a question.
!	Exclamation Mark	Indicates strong feeling.
…	Ellipsis	Shows the omission of words.
'	Apostrophe	Forms possessive or contraction.
' ' " "	Quotation Marks	Indicates material quoted. Shows emphasis.

When writing a sentence that includes a website address (URL), continue to use the appropriate punctuation. Even if the URL ends a sentence, include punctuation. In all cases, if the URL is created as a hyperlink, configure the link to exclude the punctuation, and display the punctuation directly following the link, such as that seen in the following paragraph.

You can find more information on punctuation at: en.wikipedia.org/wiki/Punctuation.

Visual Appearance

Each document should provide a consistent and pleasing look. Pay attention to the following features.

Line Justification

Ensure that vertical and horizontal line justification is consistent. Left justification is best for most business writing. Aligning material to both left and right margins generally is reserved for highly formal publications.

Headers and Footers

Ensure that headers and footers are consistent, appealing, and provide information to help your readers.

Footnotes and Endnotes

Be consistent with footnotes and endnotes. Commonly used standards include:

- *AMA Manual of Style*, www.amamanualofstyle.com (subscription required)

- *Chicago Manual of Style*, www.chicagomanualofstyle.org/ (subscription required), examples are at: write-site.athabascau.ca/example-footnotes-chicago.php

- *Oxford Guide to Style*, (free download) b-ok.cc/book/734690/6f0a3a, replaced by *New Hart's Rules*, global.oup.com/academic/product/new-harts-rules-9780199570027

- *US Government Printing Office Style Manual*, chapter 15, www.govinfo.gov/app/details/GPO-STYLEMANUAL-2016

Line Breaks

Prevent lines of text from breaking in the wrong place. For instance, numerical values and their units should stay connected and not break across two lines. Examples: *3 meters, 5 feet, 104 degrees.* If two elements like this want to break across two lines, you can force them to stay together by replacing a normal space with the ***no-break space*** character. To obtain this special character do one of the following:

- Select the no-break-space symbol from a list of special characters (such as with Microsoft Word at: ***/Insert/ Symbols/ More Symbols/ Special Characters/***)

- When using Microsoft Word, simultaneously type the control, shift, and space keys

- Enter **0160** on the numeric keypad while holding down the Alt key

In a similar fashion, prevent hyphens that tie numbers to units from breaking across two lines. Examples: *100-kph speed zone, 10-pound hammer*. To prevent a line break after the hyphen, use the ***no-break hyphen*** character. To obtain this special character:

- Select the no-break-hyphen symbol from a list of special characters

- When using Microsoft Word, simultaneously type the control, shift, and hyphen keys

- Enter **8209** on the numeric keypad while pressing the Alt key

Summary

Determine the appropriate level of proofing. Carefully scrutinize documents that will reach a wide or discerning audience.

Let your documents age before doing the final proofing.

Use a process to systematize proofreading. Use spelling and grammar checkers, but be aware that they cannot correct every problem. Also, avail yourself of text reading software to detect mistakes.

When possible, get help from another person.

Your Personal Plan

What will you do to improve your proofing skills?

On your next writing assignment, use a text reader to proof your document.

Analyze several of your documents using readability statistics. What percentage of your sentences used passive voice? What were your Flesch-Kincaid grade level scores?

Additional Resources

For more information about proofing, go to: www.toweringskills.com/7steps/more/.

Application – Preparing Informative Documents

This chapter discusses how to use the 7-step writing process to prepare informative (that is, non-fiction) documents.

I still recall the apprehension I felt 40 years ago when asked to evaluate a complex business problem and write a report recommending action. I had recently taken a new job as a young engineer at a large copper mine in Arizona. The manager asked me to examine the economic viability of two lime-burning kilns. He explained the company had decided to close a leaching plant, which consumed most of the lime from the kilns. Senior management needed to know what to do with the kilns. A take-or-pay contract supplying additional lime complicated the question.

I knew little about the lime business and less about economics. Yet, I had been assigned to find out what needed to be done and make a recommendation. The decision represented several million dollars per year and affected about 20 people, who operated the lime burning plant and the quarry supplying limestone to the kilns.

I felt trepidation not knowing how to start my investigation. How was I going to collect data, analyze it, and make a recommendation? I wasn't sure.

Nevertheless, I started asking questions and collecting data. Eventually I figured out how the company could minimize its expense. I wrote it up in a report. The manager was happy with the results. And boy was I relieved when I heard that he was satisfied.

Each new assignment to generate a report or make a presentation reminds me again that the way to overcome the angst of not knowing much about a new writing project is to get started. If you begin and keep working, everything eventually falls into place.

To help you begin some of those scary writing assignments, this chapter provides advice. You will find tips on how to prepare the documents most often required in business and other real-life situations.

Email

Email is the most prevalent type of informative writing. Surveys show that office workers typically spend 30% of their time reading and writing email.

Determine Your Purpose and Identify Your Readers

As previously discussed, before you begin writing, identify your readers and understand the purpose of your communication. Decide if email is the right media.

Would it be better to make a phone call or send a text message? People will immediately read a text message—but this is less likely with an email. On the other hand, a phone call provides instant feedback, more privacy, and greater flexibility, if the other person answers the phone. The downside of using the phone is many people fail to pick up or return phone calls.

Also, remember, email is never private. Assume that people other than your original recipients will someday read your email. In addition, an email server will retain a copy forever. If you need privacy, use the phone or talk face-to-face.

Add "To" and "Copy" Names Last

Wait to add the names of your readers to the "To" and "Copy" fields until after you write the message. This prevents sending the email prematurely.

Focus on One Topic

If you need to discuss several different subjects, send separate emails. Moreover, if your email provides different information for different recipients, consider sending separate emails with only the material relevant to each person.

Summarize Your Message in the Subject Field

Add a concise and meaningful subject line. This helps readers determine the importance of the message. Give them a reason to open your message. Remember that many business people receive as many as 100 non-spam emails each day. So help them see immediately that your email is worthwhile.

Make your subject as clear and as precise as possible. The subject line: "*Staff meeting, 2:00 PM Monday, to discuss next year's budget,*" is better than "*Important upcoming meeting.*"

Do not fill the subject line with the words *Important, Priority, Read Immediately*, etc. Rather, say what is important, such as "*Registration closes tomorrow at 5:00 PM.*"

Realize that excessively long subject lines are hard to read. From the Inbox view, smart phones truncate long subject fields, making it more difficult to understand an emails' purpose. Remember many email programs sort messages by trends, which key off the subject line. Furthermore, research shows that limiting the subject field to 7 words improves opening rates and engagement. Finally, consider how you or others will search for your message later.

Use Appropriate Salutations

For formal situations, use the common opening salutations: *Dear Mr./Ms./Mrs.* For formal closing salutations use: *Cordially, Sincerely, Warmest regards,* etc.

For more informal occasions, such as when addressing colleagues, use first names for opening and closing salutations. When repeatedly exchanging emails with close colleagues, you can drop salutations completely.

If in doubt, error on being more formal.

Identify Yourself

When sending an email to a person who does not know you, identify yourself. At the beginning of the message, start with something like, "*Dear Ms. Anson, I am Joan Pearson. Susan Zumwalt suggested that I write you ...*" Then at the end of the email, provide a text block with your name, position, company, mailing address, physical address, office phone number, cell phone number, and/or website.

Indicate If Action Is Required

State in the first paragraph if the reader needs to respond or if you are providing the email only as information. Place requests early in the message, and restate your requests at the end of the message.

Be Concise, Direct, and Polite

Use as few words as possible to provide the information requested or to ask for the help needed. Brief emails help recipients save time. In business, do not ramble or chitchat.

Be direct, but polite. Use a respectful, kind tone. People are more likely to respond to a pleasant request.

Never express anger in an email—it can come back to haunt you. When addressing conflict, refocus the conversation on constructive solutions.

When you receive a message that you feel is harsh or demanding, ask for clarification. You might write, *"What did you mean when you said ...?"* or *"I'm not sure how to read this."*

Do not prematurely take offense. Give others an opportunity to clarify their request or position. If possible, use the phone to take their comments or hear their problems. If necessary, refer complaints to persons whom the opponent respects or who has power to resolve problems.

Provide Context

When responding by email, include statements such as, *"As you requested last Thursday, concerning the product launch planned for June 5th, here are suggestions who should attend."*

Be Clear

Use short words, short sentences, and short paragraphs.

Use active voice as much as possible.

Use a simple, easy-to-read font.

Use mixed case. Do not use all lower case—it looks sloppy. In addition, do not use all upper case—it implies you are shouting or commanding. Especially in business, using all lower or upper case conveys laziness.

Use only abbreviations and acronyms that your readers readily understand.

Consider adding a simple table and/or chart with a brief explanation to summarize long, attached reports.

Organize Your Message

Break long email messages into sections. If you see that an email will run more than a few hundred words, consider replacing it with a memorandum or report.

When providing complex answers, place elements in bulleted or numbered lists.

Add Attachments Only If Necessary

Avoid attachments if you can efficiently insert the information into the email body. There is no need to send a large attachment if the reader needs only a small part of the document.

Do not send attachments unless they are specifically required. Attachments consume bandwidth, take time to open, require time to read or scan, and introduce security risks. Time-conscious and security-conscious readers will avoid or delete messages with large attachments. Also, realize that attachments often do not display well on mobile devices.

When needing to send many files or several large files use a file hosting service, such as Google Drive or Microsoft OneDrive. You can find a list of the more popular file hosting services at: en.wikipedia.org/wiki/Comparison_of_file_hosting_services.

Proofread

Carefully proof your email before sending it. Check the subject field to ensure your subject line summarizes the message and provides a reason for your readers to open the email. Activate spell-checking and grammar-checking features. Reread the message to ensure that you did not leave out words. If the email is highly important, have other persons review the email before sending it.

As already noted, add the recipients after the message is written and proofed. Double-check the recipients' field. Make sure you do not inadvertently send the document to a wrong person. Include only those recipients who need to know. And when you want recipients' names and email addresses to remain confidential, add recipients to the blind copy field.

Manage Email

Here are further suggestions regarding email:

- Respond promptly. When you receive a request for assistance, if you are too busy to help within a few hours, respond promptly by saying that you cannot help immediately and state a time when you can get to their request.

- When a person asks for free advice or free work that you cannot provide gratis, tell them politely that you cannot help them, and if possible, suggest an alternative solution, such as offering to do the work for a fee or suggesting another resource.

- Use email folders and email automation software to organize incoming email.

- To save time reading and responding to email, use the following procedures:

  o *Last in first out (LIFO)* – read the last received email first

  o *Handle only once (HOO)* – after reading an email, delete it, forward it to another person to handle, respond to it, or set it aside to handle later (only doing this for messages that you cannot delegate and that require much time)

Letters and Memos

The precursors to email—letters and memos—although used less often, still have a place. Letters and memos are useful when you need to physically deliver a message or create a stand-alone document.

Generally, you will use memos to communicate within an organization. Memos assume the readers will be familiar with the writer or unconcerned as to the identity of the writer. Therefore, you do not need to introduce yourself in a memo as you would in an email or letter written to someone who does not know you.

Most memos include fields for the subject, date, recipients (*To*), writer (*From*), and message. They typically have less than 1,000 words. Longer memos are possible, but once they get past 2 pages, a report usually will better serve the purpose. Best practice is to start long or moderate length memos with a summary and end with a conclusion.

Normally, you will send letters to individual persons. The recipients can be within or outside of the sending organization. Letters take a wide range of content and format and can be any length.

Formal letters typically start with a block of text providing contact information. This is followed by the date and an introductory salutation (*Dear Mr./Ms./...*). Formal letters end with a closing salutation (*Sincerely/Cordially/...*), the writer's signature, name, and title.

Much of the advice provided for emails applies to composing letters:

- Identify yourself at the start when writing to someone who does not know you
- Indicate if action is required
- Be direct, but polite
- Provide context
- Be concise and clear
- Organize your message with section headers if the letter is longer than one page

Reports

To keep enterprises going, managers divvy the firm's work among individuals, teams, and external service providers. The deliberations of these workers, their analyses, solutions, and plans find their way into reports.

Organizations also use reports to record decisions. This compensates for the inability of different people to remember things exactly the same. In this way, reports align institutional knowledge. If no one collects the facts and describes the analysis, the investment in collecting data and studying problems is wasted.

One more point—organizations prepare reports to communicate consistently with their customers and stakeholders.

Determine the Purpose and Identify Readers

When starting to write a report, assess the report's purpose, context, and readership. Determine the general length and complexity of the report. Decide on a format. Determine if you have sufficient information to commence work. If needed, lay out a research plan and/or get other people to help with the research and writing.

Get Started and Keep Going

As you begin, manage your emotions. It is natural to feel overwhelmed when assigned to write a long or complex report. Needing to enlist the help of other people from other departments or other companies can heighten your uneasiness, since enlisting others increases uncertainty of the timing, quality, and cost of their involvement.

When faced with a difficult report to write, it is best to jump in and start doing something as soon as possible. As you do, your feelings will change from being overwhelmed to being resigned to see the project through. And as you make measureable progress, your confidence will grow and you will acquire a hope that the assignment will turn out well. Your growing knowledge and enthusiasm will propel you through the project.

Obtain Guidance

You seldom are without a guide when writing a report. Whoever assigns or requests a report is your sponsor. Often this person is your manager or other person in charge.

When assigned a report to write, gain as full an understanding as possible of what is wanted. Do this by asking questions and taking notes.

As you advance your assignment—when your research reveals new things or when your brainstorming and organizing yields insights—check back with your sponsor to gain his or her guidance.

Invite your sponsor's advice when working outside your prior experience, facing contradictory and incomplete evidence, or dealing with weighty and emotionally charged situations. He or she likely will understand context important to your report.

Be Ethical

It is implicit that you write honestly.

Refrain from guessing. Carefully research your topic. Consult credible sources. Document where you found supporting information.

State limitations to evidence. When drafting and revising, include only validated data and relevant information. Present objective conclusions.

If you hedge the truth, you and your organization eventually will suffer the consequences for compromising your integrity.

Brainstorm, Organize, and Assemble Pre-existing Material

When you feel your research has answered the important questions, brainstorm the major ideas and organize your material into an outline. Next, bring together any text that you have already written that can be reused. Using two windows on a PC, copy sections from the already written material into the outline of the new report. This technique also works well when assembling text written by multiple authors.

Collaborate

When appropriate, get help from other people. Working with others can be challenging and time consuming, but it is imperative when writing a long and complex report.

It helps if one person manages the project and the same or another person takes the lead to assemble and wordsmith the entire document. The project manager or document editor should:

- Clearly communicate the scope, schedule, and budget of the assignment
- Define roles for the team members, including assigning portions of the document to team members according to contributors' expertise
- Establish an overall outline for the report
- Adopt standards, such as:
  - A style guide – a document that prescribes how things will be written and formatted
  - A list of abbreviations and units of measure
  - A glossary – a list of special words or terms used in the document

Standards are essential to ensure consistency and to avoid excess rewriting. Sometimes the chief editor will need to assume the role of writing instructor and educate contributors on what is and what is not effective prose.

Organize Your Material

After doing your research and brainstorming, decide how you will organize your report. As discussed in a prior chapter, common development patterns include:

- Chronology
- Spatial
- Logical
- Lists
- Problem solving
- Proposed change
- Templates specified by governments and trade associations

Select a relevant title. Add section headings. Include summary, conclusion, and recommendation sections. Use bulleted and numbered lists. Add tables, charts, illustrations, and photos. When appropriate, provide a glossary, list of abbreviations, and list of information sources. For longer reports, add finding aides, such as a table of contents, list of tables, list of figures, and/or index.

Use a minimum number of fonts. Ensure the overall document is neat and consistently formatted.

After you draft your report, during the revision phase, cycle back to check the effectiveness of the development pattern you selected and consider resequencing sections.

When your report is essentially complete, but yet unissued, obtain feedback by submitting a draft to your sponsor or to a sample set of the intended readers to obtain their comments.

Implement Revision Control

When working on a complex report, add a revision label to the file name and keep different versions. This is especially important when multiple persons edit or review a document. An effective way to do this is to add a revision letter or number to the end of the file name, such as *rev C* or *rev 03*. Use letters to indicate revisions prior to formally issuing the document and numbers to revisions that follow the formal release, with the first official issuance being *revision 00* or *edition 1*.

Avoid using the label *final* as a revision indicator, because 99% of the time what you or others think is the final revision will still require further changes. When this happens, the *final* revision is no longer final and this can create confusion. For this reason, numbers or letters make superior revision labels.

Presentations

Learning to write can help you speak before a group. Successful presentations, talks, speeches, sermons, lectures, and briefings—whether given in person or recorded—require preparation. An effective presentation is more than throwing together a deck of PowerPoint slides and reading from or talking to those slides. Rather, each good presentation starts with a well-written script.

This does not imply that all you have to do is write out a great talk and then read it in front of your audience. No. A great presentation also requires rehearsing the presentation and refining the content and the mode of delivery through practice and iterative adjustments. Without writing out what you will say and practicing, you will never hear beforehand your words and assess their effectiveness.

Prepare Your Presentation

A speaker's first mandate is to have something valuable to say. This aligns with the first three steps of the writing process:

1.   Get clear on your audience and your purpose
2.   Collect material to support your premise
3.   Brainstorm additional content

A speaker's second mandate is to engage with the audience. This requires preparing an opening that catches their interest and summarizes the presenter's message. Follow with substance that holds your audience's attention and links to their needs and desires. Include stories, share analogies, quote authorities, and cite facts. Prepare to do this by using steps 3 through 6 of the writing process, namely:

3.   Brainstorm how to effectively use your material
4.   Organize your content to hold interest and drive home your point

5.   Draft what you will say and prepare what you will show

6.   Refine what you will show and tell

Prepare a conclusion, which links back to your opening; and formulate a call to action.

Along the way, double-check your facts and thoroughly proof your slides.

Prepare Suitable Visual Aids

When preparing your script, decide on your visual aids, if any. Remember, what you will say and how you look will be far more important than a slide deck or other visual material.

When you elect to use slides, ensure that they:

- Present a clear message
- Offer benefits to the audience
- Economize on ideas and words
    - Present only one idea per slide
    - Include only the essential details
    - Include at most 6 lines per slide and 6 words per line
    - Use a large, easy-to-read font
- Use simple charts or tables to show numbers
- Employ larger font, bolding, or contrasting colors to emphasize what is most important
    - Do not overemphasize slide titles by making them too big

Slides with long sentences and small fonts cause audiences to work too hard. This stops them from reading such slides and from listening to the presenter.

When you want people to remember your message and to act on it, write a report or proposal. Deliver your presentation, and then hand out the report or proposal. A written report will accomplish more to encourage action and enable people to remember what you said than any slide deck. Moreover, a business proposal distributed at the end of a presentation offers many opportunities for you and your team to follow up with your audience.

Practice

Once you have finalized what you will say and show, rehearse your presentation until you can present it naturally and with only a few notes. Your goal is to deliver it without reading it word for word. Rarely is an improvised talk as good as a well-prepared presentation that is read; but best of all is a well-prepared and well-rehearsed presentation.

Practice your presentation by standing up and reading your script aloud again and again with the expression, tone, and body language you plan to use. As you do, you will find portions of your presentation that need changing. Some of your words and phrases will seem unnatural. Some of your ideas will be unclear or weak. Improve them.

Spread out your practice. This will enable you to internalize your material and ultimately deliver it with more confidence.

As you progress, bring in a colleague or two to critique your content and presentation techniques. Be open to their comments and make changes.

Prepare for Questions

Anticipate questions from your audience, and write out answers. Keep these in reserve until needed.

Control Your Emotions

When the time comes to deliver your presentation, relax. It is normal to feel anxiety standing in front of a group of people. To control nervousness, focus on your audience and your message. If you have prepared a great message and practiced delivering it, you will be confident. And this confidence will show.

Be authentic. Present your genuine character and a true message.

Be charitable. Wish the best for your audience and for others.

Be vulnerable. Be open to questions and criticism.

Control Your Looks

Consider your dress, grooming, posture, facial features, eye contact, and hand gestures.

How you look will influence your perceived authority, competence, and humanity. As you walk on the stage or move to the front of a conference room, your audience will size you up. They will judge your credibility before you begin talking. So, consider your audience, as you select your clothing and grooming.

In addition, maintain an upright posture and project a friendly face. To prepare for this, before you speak, relax your body by taking several deep breaths, by stretching your arms and legs, and by slowly moving your head from side to side and nodding up and down to stretch the muscles in your neck. However, do this in private or inconspicuously.

When speaking in a conference room, stand up and move to the front of the room. Do not stay seated in your chair. Do not lean against the wall. Do not sit on the edge of a desk or table.

Face the audience. Stand with the projector screen, white board, or easel to your left. Use your left hand, with the palm open and facing the audience, to point to important points on your visuals. Doing this allows your audience to look at you and then sweep their eyes to their right to your slides. This is the normal eye movement for speakers of English and most other languages. (If you are presenting in Arabic, Hebrew, Persian, or other languages where word flow is right-to-left, stand on the opposite side of the presentation.)

When talking, if possible, move around in a natural way. Stand straight, but not rigidly.

If using a podium, stand behind it, but do not touch it. Let your hands hang loose. This prevents you from clutching or leaning on the podium. In addition, it frees your hands so you can make hand gestures.

If not using a podium, also let your arms and hands extend to your sides when not using them to gesture.

Smile—make it natural. You do not have to smile constantly. Rather, smile from time to time, when your message indicates a smile is appropriate.

Make eye contact. Effective eye contact conveys honesty and authority. When standing before a group, look squarely at one person for several seconds. Hold this eye contact until you complete a sentence. Then move to another person. In a 10-minute presentation to 30 people, you should be able to look at every person several times. As you proceed, bounce around the room—do not move person by person in a row as if knocking down aligned dominoes. Obviously, if you are speaking to 100 or more people, you cannot look everyone in the eye, but moving to different parts of the room will convey the impression that you are looking at everyone.

When making hand gestures keep your hands at your chest or head level so they are more visible.

Control How You Sound

Speak up. Provide volume, especially when on stage or in a large room.

If using a microphone, arrive before your talk early enough so you can test the best place to position the microphone stand or to hold the mic. When public speaking, the best mic position is a few inches in front of your mouth at a 45° angle. This enables the mic to capture your voice while leaving the view of your face mostly unobstructed.

When testing a mic, have another person check the sound of your voice throughout the room.

Speak distinctly. Annunciate every syllable.

As you speak, vary your volume to match the words. Increasing the volume communicates authority, while reducing the volume generates a feeling of intimacy or suspense.

Control the pitch of your voice. When you are nervous or excited, the pitch of your voice naturally increases. To project confidence, relax your voice and drop the pitch.

Vary your pace. Speak quickly to create excitement or when presenting many details that are subordinate to your main point. Speak slowly when you want to emphasize words and items. A complete pause of several seconds can add huge emphasis.

Cut out *uh, um*, false starts, and other speech disfluencies. They kill credibility. If you need to collect your thoughts, pause.

Control your tone by controlling how you feel. It is possible to speak the same words but vary the tone to create a wide range of feelings—spanning from joy to sorrow, sincerity to sarcasm, and excitement to apathy. Do this by consciously feeling an emotion and then inflecting your voice to match that emotion.

To be effective, you will need to practice these techniques when rehearsing.

Other Tips

Arrive early at your venue. Use this time not only to check the microphone and audio system, but also to get familiar with the room and/or stage. If appropriate, meet and briefly interact with a portion of the audience as they enter the room.

After your presentation, if appropriate, linger and talk with those who have questions or comments. This is a good way to make useful contacts.

Articles, Blogs, and Websites

Articles are vital to our lives. We read them to learn the news, to find answers to questions, to solve problems, and to be entertained. They occur as webpages, blogs, e-zines, newsletters, newspapers, magazines, and technical journals. We find them on line, embedded in email, and printed on paper.

Today, if you want to be read, you need not be a prominent author, nor represent a name brand. You need only to write something interesting and place it before likeminded readers. However, writing well will increase your readership and your influence.

Having Something to Say

Great articles begin with memorable ideas. For your material to standout, it must be:

- Relevant
- Unique
- Honest
- Substantial

Readers find articles striking if the pieces solve their problems or address their interests. To be relevant, your material must be useful—even if the only use is to entertain.

Articles need to provide unique information. The ideas need to differ from the knowledge readers already possess.

Your readers want to know that information comes from reliable sources. Therefore, provide proof—share the results of studies, include testimonials, and cite sources.

The information needs to be more than trivial. To have substance, your pieces must address specific problems and provide step-by-step solutions or they should address special interests in a substantial way. To find their way into top-ranking search engine results, articles published on the internet generally should be 2,000-5,000 words.

Select an Attention-Getting Headline

Start with a strong title that both captures readers' attention and summarizes the article. Typically, the title will include a short main headline and a longer sub-headline.

Match the length of your title to your media and purpose. Research shows the optimum title length for online articles is:[19]

- Business-to-consumer (B2C) articles – 12-18 words
- Business-to-business (B2B) articles – 6-12 words
- Online newspapers – 8 words

Generally, titles of printed newspapers and magazines are shorter, being 3-9 words.[20] With trade journals, some of the most attention-gaining titles are as short as one word, especially when they link to current events or topics with high interest.

Test what works for your situation.

In addition, research on internet articles shows that the first 2-3 words and last 2-3 words in a headline are the most important, because they are the words most often read when quickly scanned.[21]

Write It Well

Once you have selected memorable content and a strong headline, use effective writing techniques to present the material. Use words that your readers use to describe the topic. Generally, these words should rank high for search engine optimization (SEO) for your topic.

Provide a strong first paragraph. Grab the readers' attention. Then, continue to hold that attention through the body of the article. Finally, add a conclusion, enumerate recommendations, and make a call to action.

Make sure that your logic is valid. Safeguard that your document holds together by checking to see that every part contributes to the central message.

Include stories and analogies to strengthen your premise. Add images and media. But add only material that advances your purpose and provides value.

Write in a familiar tone. Use short words, short sentences, and short paragraphs. Strive to achieve a natural flow by adding words and phrases to transition from one idea to the next.

Technical articles require a more formal tone, and they use larger and more complex words, but they still should have a comfortable flow. When writing technical articles, replace categorical writing with analytical writing and use active voice as much as possible.

Make articles visually appealing. Add headers throughout your documents so readers can quickly scan for content. Use bulleted and numbered lists. Use an easy-to-read font. Ensure that images, graphs, and tables are consistently formatted. Provide white space.

Proof the document for missing words, punctuation, spelling, and grammar.

Business Proposals

A business proposal or sales proposal is a written offer to provide a service or product. Proposals are crucial to complex or high-priced sales.

The length and complexity of a proposal varies with the cost and intricacy of the offering. Proposals for simple services can be as short as one or two pages, while proposals for large construction projects can have hundreds of pages, often including many large volumes of supplemental information. Similar to other writing tasks, it is important to understand the reader and the purpose of the proposal.

Sophisticated buyers typically provide requests for proposals (RFPs) when bidding for work that is difficult to estimate or for work that will be on going, and they typically provide requests for quotations (RFQs) when seeking to buy a piece of equipment or contract a job that is well defined.

Buyers generally award bids for well-defined scope primarily on price. In contrast, awards for difficult-to-define scope stress professional qualifications and the organizational fit to the buyer's needs.

Unsolicited proposals differ remarkably from solicited proposals. Unsolicited proposals attempt to awaken potential buyers to unrecognized risks and unspotted opportunities.

Gather Information

Information gathering always precedes the preparation of a proposal. Sales organizations gather information from the documents and instructions buyers supply—requests for proposals, specifications, and bid meetings—and from talking with decision makers and with those who influence the buying decision.

An effective proposal requires a thorough understanding of the buyer's:

1. Pain (the acknowledged problems)
2. Need for a solution
3. Estimate of the value of a solution
4. Assessment of an acceptable budget to obtain a solution

To be ethical, when receiving a solicitation for a proposal, providers of goods and services can only gather information through formal channels. These include the request for proposal, documents appended to it, pre-bid meetings hosted by the soliciting organization, and authorized question-asking mechanisms.

On the other hand, informal or unsolicited proposals enable the supplier to ask for information through many informal channels. When anticipating an important solicitation, a supplier should talk to the customer before the request for proposal is prepared. Through informal conversations, the supplier should learn the answers to the four previously listed items and quantified the value the buyer places on a solution.

Examples of questions the supplier can ask to obtain this information include:

- What are the major issues challenging your organization?
- Help me understand what you mean when you say your organization "is failing to ..."

- What have you previously attempted to do to address this problem?
- What do you think you can do to eliminate this problem?
- What are your criteria for a successful solution?
- What other concerns do you have?
- What concerns do others in your organization have?
- What are the primary concerns of your management?
- What does this problem cost you?
- How much is this problem costing your organization?
- What would it be worth to your organization if you could …?
- If you could save a million dollars per year, what type of budget would your organization be willing to commit to a solution?
- If you could achieve …, what would it be worth to your organization?
- What type of funding is available to address these problems/opportunities/situations?
- What would be the compelling reasons for senior management to agree to a project that would …?
- Who in your organization can approve this type of project?
- What issues could sidetrack this type of project?

When asking questions, it is important for the seller to listen carefully to the buyer. The insight obtained from truly listening to the buyer and understanding his or her problems can provide the extra perception to write a proposal that is more compelling.

The seller should gather this intelligence from both decision makers and from technical experts who will evaluate the proposal in detail and make recommendations to the decision makers.

Draft and Refine the Proposal

With this essential knowledge in hand, the proposal writer crafts an offer that:

- States the buyer's objectives
- Restates the value of achieving the objectives

- Proposes a range of options to achieve the objectives—the best practice is to offer three options, with the range including low, mid, and high cost offers
- Includes language and a signature acceptance field for the buyer, so the proposal can serve as a purchase order or contract

Follow the outline provided by the request for proposal, use a template provided by your firm, or adopt one from the many available on the internet. Format the document in a common font. Define sections with headers for each. Include a table of contents. Describe key terms and include a glossary if the document is long and the material is complex—this will be useful to purchasing personnel and the ultimate decision maker, who may be less familiar with industry jargon. Also, clarify terms that you use in a unique way.

Use a cover letter and the proposal summary to pitch your solution to the organization's pain. Do not waste this highly visible part of a report droning on and on about the extensive experience and sterling qualities of your organization. Rather, focus on the buyer's problems and on your proposal's ability to economically solve them.

Use bullet lists, tables, and charts to make your proposal clear, concise, and readable. Use direct, but familiar language.

In the body of the proposal, describe in detail the buyer's problems and provide defensible evidence of the value of the proposed solutions. Provide a detailed description of the service and/or products that you will provide and how they address the buyer's problems and issues. Quantify the resources and time needed to develop the solution. For complex proposals this will include milestone dates, a project schedule (Gant chart), and cost estimate or bill of materials that build to a quotation/budget.

Some proposals will provide budgetary estimates with payments linked to actual costs, while other proposals will include lump-sum bids to do all of the work described by the scope.

Describe the payment terms, such as *"25% payment due on signing"* and *"fee of 1% per month charged on payments made 30 days after billing."* For large and complex projects, this language can be extensive.

Prepare a Work Plan

Many buyers will prepare a written scope of work (SOW) to describe the goods and services to fulfill a request for quotation (RFQ) or request for proposal (RFP). The scope of work is a detailed list of goods and services to meet the buyer's objective. On the other hand, less sophisticated buyers may communicate only verbally their objectives.

The supplier translates the buyer's objectives and the scope of work into a project plan. Such a plan defines in detail who does what when where how and why:

- What services and/or products will be prepared and/or delivered? This is the scope of work.

- What resources (persons, departments, and subcontractors) will do the work to build and deliver the services and/or products?

- When will the work begin and end? What are other milestone dates? This is the schedule.

- Where will the work occur and where will the services and/or products be delivered?

- How will the resources work to prepare the product and/or service? Who will manage the effort? How will the supplier ensure quality, timely delivery, and budget compliance?

- Why are you recommending this range of solutions to the customer? This is the justification.

Preparing this information for large projects typically requires project management and professional cost estimating. A typical approach is to create a work breakdown structure (WBS), which is an organization of the project deliverables into smaller components. For instance, with the construction of a building, there is the foundation, walls, roof, piping, electrical, and painting. Within each group, there will be further divisions, such as the foundation being divided into excavation, forms, concrete, and reinforcing steel. This breakdown continues to smaller and smaller elements until each element is manageable as an individual work package.

Follow a Template

Sophisticated buyers typically specify in their request for proposals the arrangement of proposal elements. Bidders should meticulously follow such guidelines. When the buyers do not specify the content and format, a good pattern is:

- Cover letter
  - ○ Summarize the buyer's problems or the opportunities available to the buyer.
  - ○ State the value the solution or opportunity provides the buyer.
  - ○ Show how the supplier is uniquely qualified to provide the most economical or most valuable solution. Briefly mention similar problems you have solved for other buyers.
  - ○ Describe guarantees or other risk mitigation that will minimize the buyer's risks.
  - ○ Make a call to action. Ask for prompt approval to proceed.
  - ○ Do not waste this space by talking excessively about your company in an aggrandizing manner—rather focus on the buyer's pain (problems) and how you will provide relief (solutions).
  - ○ Provide personal contact information so readers can reach you immediately if they have questions.
- Front material
  - ○ Add a title page, table of contents, list of figures, list of tables, and list of abbreviations.
- Summary or executive summary
  - ○ Write the summary similar to the cover letter.
  - ○ Discuss the buyer's problems or missed opportunities.
  - ○ Summarize several options for addressing the problem.
  - ○ Link the seller's strengths to the buyer's problems. In addition, show that the seller can provide the best solutions.
  - ○ Summarize the project's economics.
  - ○ Create a compelling case for the buyer to move ahead immediately with one of your proposed solutions.

- Assessment
  - Describe the buyer's needs and/or opportunities and the value of a solution. Quantify the value of a solution.
  - Explain the context of the problems.
  - Discuss prior attempts (if any) to solve the problems and explain why those efforts failed.
- Solution/Plan/Project
  - Propose a range of solutions to the problems or concisely describe the project.
  - Describe the work to be done. List deliverables and delivery dates.
  - Offer alternatives.
  - Anticipate questions and objections from members of the buyer's team and include material that answers potential questions and negates possible objections.
- Schedule
  - Provide project milestones and a detailed schedule (if appropriate).
- Qualifications
  - Describe the delivery organization or team. Summarize the supplier's experience and capacity relevant to the plan. Stress unique capabilities and strengths of your organization or team. Link these strengths to the project.
  - Include profiles of key team members.
- Budget/Pricing/Cost
  - Summarize elements of the scope and provide the cost for each element.
  - Explain assumptions.
- Economics/Cost-Benefit Analysis
  - List the project benefits, quantifying each item.
  - Compare the total financial value of the benefits to the cost. If possible, provide discounted cash flow calculations with common economic indicators—internal rate of return (IRR), net present value (NPV), benefit-cost ratio (BCR), and earnings before interest, tax, depreciation, and amortization (EBITDA).

- Conclusion
  - Restate the buyer's problems or opportunities.
  - Restate the range of solutions.
  - Restate the advantages the seller possesses to provide the solutions.
  - Restate the project economic benefits.
  - Provide a call to action. Ask for prompt approval. Include a deadline stating when your proposal expires.
- Terms & Conditions
  - Describe terms, conditions, and assumptions. Specify the duration of the agreement, reiterate the overall timetable for completion, specify payment dates and payment methods, state how the proposal can be amended, etc. It is likely that your supply or legal department will provide this section.
- Acceptance/Approval
  - Provide a field at the end of the document where the buyer can sign and date the document and select solution options. This will enable the supplier to begin work immediately on the project, when the buyer signs and returns the document.
- Appendices
  - Add a detailed schedule.
  - Include a financial model used to estimate project economics.
  - Provide background on the supplier's organization, such as similar past projects.
  - Attach resumes of key team members.

Proof

Carefully proofread the proposal. Pay especial attention to the bid pricing, budget, and financial analysis. Ensure that repetitions of key numbers are consistent throughout the document and the cover letter.

Summary

While there are many more types of informative writing, these are the common ones. With each type of document, adequate prewriting, rapid drafting, thorough rewriting, and careful proofreading will lead to strong documents and solid results.

Your Personal Plan

What important documents are on your horizon?

How can you apply the principles from this chapter to improve what you are writing?

Additional Resources

For videos and more information on preparing informative documents, go to: www.toweringskills.com/7steps/more/.

Afterword

We live in the Information Age. Essentially an unlimited amount of information is available to much of the earth's population. In a world becoming increasingly interlinked and data-rich, individuals and organizations gain a competitive advantage by producing superior documents. Not only do well-written documents help us communicate more effectively, but the labor of writing and rewriting them helps us think clearly.

As you seek to improve your writing, start with a proven writing process. Advance one step at a time, learning and applying the skills to everyday writing tasks. Whatever you write—emails, text messages, reports, proposals, scripts, web pages, or blog posts—make them the best you can.

Get clear about your readers and your theme. Collect the information needed to support your position. Expand your thinking through brainstorming. Make mind maps and outlines to organize your content. Draft quickly. Edit for clarity, brevity, and a natural flow. Embrace the full power of word processing and grammar checking. Enlist the aid of an electronic text reader. In summary, work hard at your writing so your readers do not have to work hard at reading what you write.

Most of all, take pride in what you write. It reflects on your mind and character. It is an important asset.

As you strive to write better, I wish you much success.

Your Personal Plan

What are you going to do to be a better writer?

Additional Resources

For additional writing tips see: www.toweringskills.com.

Appendix – Words People Confuse

This section lists commonly confused English words. It provides pronunciations, explains differences in meaning, and shows examples of the words used correctly. Many of these words are homonyms, that is, words with the same sound, but different meanings.

Pronunciations are general American English and use the *New Oxford American Dictionary* (NOAD) phonetic key explained at: en.wikipedia.org/wiki/Pronunciation_respelling_for_English. Both Google and Bing use this phonetic key.

accent, ascent, assent
/ˈakˌsent/, /əˈsent/, /əˈsent/

As a verb, *accent* means to emphasize or give importance. As a noun, *accent* is the stress given to certain syllables in spoken language. *Accent* is also the mark used to indicate that stress. *Ascent* is a noun meaning an upward journey. As a verb, *assent* means to agree. As a noun, *assent* means agreement.

Example: *The captain placed a strong <u>accent</u> on the word "go" as he commanded, "Let's go!" This indicated his hearty <u>assent</u> to make an <u>ascent</u> of the hill.*

accept, except
/əkˈsept/, /ikˈsept/

Accept is a verb meaning to receive or to allow. As a verb, *except* means to exclude. In addition, *except* is often used as a preposition or as a conjunction to indicate exclusion.

Example: *Joan will <u>accept</u> the assignment <u>except</u> task 3. She intends to <u>except</u> herself from that portion of the project.*

adverse, averse
/adˈvərs,ˈadˌvərs/, /əˈvərs/

Adverse is an adjective meaning unfavorable or contrary. *Averse* is an adjective meaning having a strong dislike or opposition.

Example: *Mary is <u>averse</u> to John's plan, because she believes it will have an <u>adverse</u> effect on morale.*

advice, advise

/əd'vīs/, /əd'vīz/

Advice is a noun meaning counsel or a recommendation. *Advise* is a verb meaning to recommend or to inform.

Example: *Edward advised Joy to take the police officer's advice.*

affect, affect, effect

/ə'fekt/, /'afekt/, /ə'fekt/

Generally used as a verb, *affect* (/ə'fekt/) means to influence, to make a difference, or to pretend. *Affect* (/'afekt/) is used only as a noun in formal English as a technical term in psychology meaning a feeling or emotion as distinguished from a thought. As a verb in formal English, *effect* means to make, to do, or to accomplish. Generally used as a noun, *effect* means a result or consequence.

Example: *Adam's statements will affect his children, who affect indifference. This is the effect of his love. Hopefully, it will effect peace.*

aide, aid

/ād/, /ād/

Aide is a noun meaning a person who assists. As a noun, *aid* means help or assistance; and as a verb, *aid* means to assist or help.

Example: *The charity provides aid to those in need. In this context, the chairman's aide helped the refugee find the staff member empowered to aid those with immigration issues.*

all ready, already

/ôl 'redē/, /ˌôl'redē/

All ready is an adjective phrase meaning totally prepared. *Already* is an adverb indicating before.

Example: *Brian was all ready for the trip. In fact, he had already saddled his horse.*

all together, altogether

/ôl tə'geT͟Hər/, /ˌôltə'geT͟Hər/

All together is an adjective or adverb phrase that means in a group. *Altogether* is an adverb meaning totally or completely.

Example: *The weekend spent all together proved altogether fun.*

allusive, elusive, illusive
/əˈlo͞osiv,əˈlo͞oziv/, /ēˈlo͞osiv/, /iˈlo͞osiv/

All three words are adjectives. *Allusive* means indirect. *Allusive* is related to the noun *allusion*, which means an indirect but meaningful reference. *Elusive* means evasive or difficult to capture, find, describe, or remember. *Elusive* is related to the verb *elude*, meaning to evade or avoid. *Illusive* means being deceived or believing in something unreal or unreachable. *Illusive* is related to the noun *illusion*, which is something that appears real, but is not.

Example: *The solution to the differential equation proved elusive, because the professor's suggestion proved worse than allusive; in fact, his hint was deceptive. Justifiably, the students felt deceived by his illusive suggestion.*

altar, alter
/ˈôltər/, /ˈôltər/

Altar is a noun meaning a sacred table or raised spot. *Alter* is a verb meaning to change.

Example: *The sign reads "Please do not alter the altar."*

among, between
/əˈməNG/, /bəˈtwēn/

Among is an adverb meaning in the company of a group. *Between* generally is a preposition meaning at, into, or across the space separating two (and only two) objects or places. *Between* also can be an adverb with the same sense of separating two things.

Example: *On her expedition in the Amazon, between the coast and the river, the scientist found several new species among the many insects she collected.*

anecdote, antidote
/ˈanəkˌdōt/, /ˈan(t)iˌdōt/

Anecdote is a noun meaning a short, interesting story about a person or event. *Antidote* is a noun meaning a medicine use to counteract a poison or a similar intervention to improve a bad situation.

Example: *The nurse told a charming <u>anecdote</u> of her administering an <u>antidote</u> to a grouchy patient.*

appraise, apprise

/əˈprāz/, /əˈprīz/

Appraise is a verb meaning to estimate the value. *Apprise* is a verb meaning to tell or inform.

Example: *Carla <u>apprised</u> the homebuyer that the appraiser would <u>appraise</u> the house by the end of the week.*

arbiter, arbitrator

/ˈärbədər/, /ˈärbəˌtrādər/

An *arbiter* is a noun meaning a person who resolves a dispute or who has ultimate authority over a matter. An *arbitrator* is a noun meaning an impartial person or organization selected to settle a dispute.

Examples: *James disliked the <u>arbitrator</u>'s decision; therefore, he reluctantly agreed to leave the outcome in the hands of God, whom he regarded as the true <u>arbiter</u> of right and wrong.*

a while, awhile

/əˈ(h)wīl/, /əˈ(h)wīl/

A while is a noun phrase meaning a period of time, while *awhile* is an adverb meaning for a short period of time.

Example: *Walk with me <u>awhile</u>. I need <u>a while</u> to adjust to your being home.*

bare, bear

/ber/, /ber/

As a verb, *bare* means to uncover or expose. As an adjective, *bare* means uncovered or exposed. As a noun, *bear* is a large mammal of the animal family Ursidae. As a verb, *bear* means to give birth, endure, tolerate, support, carry, or turn.

Example: *During the winter, when the chill wind has stripped <u>bare</u> the branches of the oak trees, the she-<u>bear</u> will <u>bear</u> her cubs. <u>Bear</u> in mind, for now, she is a solitary black <u>bear</u>, <u>barely</u> able to <u>bear</u> the company of other members of her species.*

berth, birth
/bərTH/, /bərTH/

Berth is a noun meaning a place to rest. As a noun, *birth* indicates the start of life. As a verb, *birth* means to give life to a baby or young animal.

Example: *The seal gave birth to the pup on the rocky berth.*

beside, besides
/bə'sīd/, /bə'sīdz/

Beside is a preposition meaning next to. *Besides* generally is an adverb meaning in addition.

Example: *Besides wanting a snack, Lucas wants to sit beside his grandmother.*

bolder, boulder
/'bōldər/, /'bōldər/

Bolder is an adjective meaning more confident, more vivid, or stronger. A *boulder* is a noun meaning a large rock.

Example: *The artist painted the picture in bolder colors, while he sat on a boulder.*

born, borne
/bôrn/, /bôrn/

Born is the past participle of the verb *bear* meaning to give birth. In addition, *born* is an adjective indicating the existence because of birth of a person, animal, or concept. *Borne* is a past participle of the verb *bear* and means carried, supported, endured, or tolerated.

Example: *Jane is a born optimist. She was born during April, when the ice was borne away by the flooding river.*

brake, break
/brāk/, /brāk/

As a verb, *brake* means to stop or to decrease the speed of motion. As a noun, *brake* carries a similar sense of something that slows or stops. *Break* as a verb means to divide or make unworkable. As a noun, *break* means an interruption, discontinuity, pause, gap, or a sudden fortunate opportunity. *Break* when used with helper words creates many idiomatic expressions, such as, *break away, break cover, break down, break even, break in, break new ground, break off, hell breaks loose, break the ice, break out*, etc.

Example: *Please break your habit of always braking so quickly. You are wearing out my car brakes, breaking my patience, and letting all hell break loose with the contents of my glove box. If you stop it now, I'll give you a break from my complaining.*

broach, brooch
/brōCH/, /brōCH/

Broach is a verb meaning to raise a sensitive subject for discussion. **Brooch** is a noun meaning an ornament fastened to clothing.

Examples: *Maria broached the topic with her sister, telling her, "Your brooch doesn't match your earrings."*

canvas, canvass
/ˈkanvəs/, /ˈkanvəs/

As a noun, *canvas* is a strong, course cloth. As a verb, *canvas* means to cover with a strong, course cloth. As a verb, *canvass* means to ask for votes or to gather opinions. As a noun, *canvass* means the action of asking for votes or gathering opinions.

Example: *The politician canvassed the county seeking support. Often he spoke from a canvas-covered platform attached to the back of an old pickup truck.*

censor, censure, sensor
/ˈsensər/, /ˈsen(t)SHər/, /ˈsensər/

As a verb, *censor* means to examine and to suppress unacceptable parts of a letter, book, movie, or other written or recorded communication. As a noun, *censor* is the person who examines and suppresses unacceptable parts of written or recorded material. As a verb, *censure* means to express strong disapproval. As a noun, *censure* is an expression of disapproval. *Sensor* is a noun that indicates a device for detecting or measuring physical properties.

Example: *The military officer censored the journal article, because it revealed sensitive information concerning a night-vision motion sensor. The officer also censured the author who wrote the article.*

capital, capitol
/ˈkapədl/, /ˈkapədl/

As a noun, *capital* means the leading city of a state or nation, a sum of money, the top of a stone column, or an upper case letter. As an adjective, *capital* means most important or serious. *Capitol* is a domed building or group of buildings used for government.

Example: *The US Senate meets in the* <u>Capitol</u>, *which is located on* <u>Capitol</u> *Hill, this being an important neighborhood in our nation's* <u>capital</u> *and the center of huge* <u>capital</u> *spending.*

choose, chose
/CHo͞oz/, /CHōz/

Choose is a verb indicating to select, where *choose* is the present tense and *chose* is the past tense.

Example: *Today I will* <u>choose</u> *buttermilk donuts. Yesterday, I* <u>chose</u> *raisin muffins.*

cite, sight, site
/sīt/, /sīt/, /sīt/

The verb *cite* means to quote or reference. The noun *sight* is something seen, something worth seeing, or a person's ability to see. The noun *site* is a location.

Example: *I* <u>cite</u> *the record, even though it originates from a* <u>site</u> *where many people have lost* <u>sight</u> *of the truth.*

coarse, course
/kôrs/, /kôrs/

The adjective *coarse* means large in size, rough in texture, or vulgar in manners. The noun *course* means a path or plan, such as a course of study or education. The phrase *of course* is an idiomatic adverbial phrase meaning naturally, as planned, or as expected

Example: *Of* <u>course</u>, *the history* <u>course</u> *describes the* <u>course</u> *followed by the army, which included a highway covered with* <u>coarse</u> *gravel.*

145

complement, compliment

/ˈkämpləmənt/, /ˈkämpləmənt/

Complement is a verb meaning to match or supplement. As a noun, it has the same sense. *Compliment* is a verb meaning to praise or congratulate; and as a noun, it has the same sense.

Example: *Compliment your host, so that gratitude will complement your humility.*

conscience, conscious

/ˈkänSHəns/, /ˈkänSHəs/

Conscience is a noun indicating a person's thoughts about right and wrong. *Conscious* is an adjective indicating sensibility or awareness of one's surroundings.

Example: *Jane was conscious that her conscience was free of worry.*

consul, council, counsel

/ˈkänsəl/, /ˈkounsəl/, /ˈkounsəl/

A *consul* is a noun indicating an office of government. *Council* is a noun indicating a group who confers together. *Counsel* is a noun meaning advice or a person who gives advice, such as a lawyer or barrister. *Counsel* is also a verb meaning to give advice or talk with others.

Example: *The German consul met members of the Council on Foreign Relations seeking counsel to console the prime minister, who had been alarmed by high-priced counsel.*

datum, data

/ˈdādəm,ˈdadəm/, /ˈdadə,ˈdādə/

Datum is a noun meaning one piece of information, such as a number, while *data* is the plural form of *datum*. Modern usage has grown to accept *data* as a singular noun meaning a collection of facts.

Example: *The data are correct, now that John corrected the bad datum. This caused Mary to say, "The data is now OK."*

decent, descent, dissent

/ˈdēs(ə)nt/, /dəˈsent/, /dəˈsent/

Decent is an adjective meaning good or wholesome. **Descent** is a noun meaning the action to go down or the origin of a person in terms of genealogy or ethnicity. **Dissent** is a noun meaning disagreement.

Example: *Smith is a decent fellow of German descent. However, he expressed his dissent with the ruling, which allows descent of commercial aviation to 5,000 feet over the city.*

desert, deserts, deserts, dessert

/ˈdezərt/, /ˈdezərts/, /dəˈzərts/, /dəˈzərt/

As a singular noun, **desert** (/ˈdezərt/) means a dry place, and as a plural noun, **deserts** (/ˈdezərts/) means several dry places, while **deserts** (/dəˈzərts/) means a person's entitlement to punishment or reward. As a verb, **desert** (/dəˈzərt/) means to abandon. **Dessert** (/dəˈzərt/) is sweet food, typically served at the end of a meal.

Example: *While visiting the desert of Arizona, I ate a lot of frozen desserts. Because I deserted (abandoned) my diet, I put on a lot of weight, which was my just deserts (punishment).*

device, devise

/dəˈvīs/, /dəˈvīz/

Device is a noun meaning a tool or instrument. **Devise** is a verb meaning to prepare or fix.

Example: *Please devise a device to help people eliminate this divisive practice.*

discreet, discrete

/diˈskrēt/, /diˈskrēt/

Both words are adjectives. **Discreet** means careful with what one says or does. **Discrete** means separate or distinct.

Example: *Diane used discreet language to describe the discrete events.*

disburse, disperse

/dis'bərs/, /də'spərs/

Disburse is a verb meaning to distribute money. As a verb, *disperse* means to spread out over a large area or throughout a large space. As an adjective, *disperse* is the quality of being widely distributed.

Example: *The controller <u>disbursed</u> the monthly payments to the chemical lab, which was investigating how to better <u>disperse</u> oil in water.*

dominant, dominate

/'dämənənt/, /'dämə,nāt/

Dominant is an adjective that means most important or influential. *Dominate* is a verb meaning to exercise control or to be the most conspicuous.

Example: *The most <u>dominant</u> species <u>dominate</u> the habitat.*

dual, duel

/'do͞oəl/, /'do͞oəl/

Dual generally is an adjective indicating two. *Duel* is a noun meaning a formal match or fight.

Example: *The <u>duel</u> served <u>dual</u> purposes: striking down the villain and freeing the oppressed.*

dyeing, dying

/'dīiNG/, /'dīiNG/

Both words are verbs. *Dyeing* means to apply a color through soaking in a liquid. *Dying* means giving up or losing life.

Example: *Your hair is <u>dying</u>, because you are <u>dyeing</u> it too much.*

elicit, illicit

/ē'lisət/, /i(l)'lisit/

Elicit is a verb meaning to cause or provoke. *Illicit* is an adjective meaning illegal.

Example: *Cheating can <u>elicit</u> other <u>illicit</u> activities.*

eligible, illegible

/ˈeləjəb(ə)l/, /i(l)ˈlejəb(ə)l/

Both words are adjectives. *Eligible* means suitable. *Illegible* means unreadable.

Example: *The teacher told Jacob that he was not <u>eligible</u> for recess, because his report was <u>illegible</u>.*

eminent, imminent

/ˈemənənt/, /ˈimənənt/

Both words are adjectives. *Eminent* means prominent or important. *Imminent* means soon to happen.

Example: *The <u>eminent</u> astronomer predicted an <u>imminent</u> solar eclipse.*

ensure, insure

/inˈSHŏŏr, enˈSHŏŏr/, /inˈSHŏŏr/

Both words are verbs. *Ensure* means to assure or reassure. *Insure* means to financially protect.

Example: *A person should <u>ensure</u> that they have insurance from a sound company that <u>insures</u> against losses. When insurance companies <u>insure</u> their clients against losses, they generate emotional security among their clients, which <u>ensures</u> mutual success.*

fair, fare

/fer/, /fer/

As an adjective, *fair* means equal, reasonable, or equitable. As a noun, *fair* means a gathering to share merchandise or advice. *Fare* is a noun meaning a fee or payment.

Example: *The airline charged a <u>fair fare</u> for people attending the Biggin Hill International Air <u>Fair</u>.*

farther, further

/ˈfärTHər/, /ˈfərTHər/

As adjectives and adverbs, *farther* and *further* have the common meaning of being at or extending over a greater distance. *Further* also means additional or more advanced. And, as a verb, *further* means to promote or to develop.

Example: *The further I think on your advice, the more I am inclined to further the argument that he should move farther away from the highway.*

flaunt, flout
/flônt,flänt/, /flout/

Flaunt is a verb meaning to show off. **Flout** is a verb meaning to disregard a rule or social convention.

Example: *The maid flouted the house rules by taking a photo with her smart phone of the actress flaunting a large pearl necklace.*

forbear, forebear
/fər'ber, fôr'ber/, /'fôrber/

Forbear is a verb meaning to restrain an impulse. **Forebear** is a noun meaning an ancestor.

Example: *Please forbear talking further about your repugnant forebear.*

formally, formerly
/'fôrməlē/, /'fôrmərlē/

Both words are adverbs. **Formally** means rigidly. **Formerly** means before.

Example: *The firm formally resolved to abandon practices that formerly proved dangerous.*

forth, fourth
/fôrTH/, /fôrTH/

Forth is an adverb meaning forward. **Fourth** is the ordinal number associated with the cardinal number four (4).

Example: *Proceed forth to the fourth block, turn right, then proceed forth another four blocks.*

gibe, gybe, jibe, jive
/jīb/, /jīb/, /jīb/, /jīv/

As nouns, **gibe** and **jibe** both mean an insult or a taunt; and as verbs, **gibe** and **jibe** mean to insult or mock. As verbs **jibe** and **gybe** mean to change the course of a ship by shifting the sail to the other side of the vessel; and as nouns, *jibe* and *gybe* mean the act of making such a change in the sails. *Jibe*, used as a verb, also means to agree. As a noun, *jive* means a lively type of dancing popular in the 1940s and 1950s or lively, meaningless talking. As a verb, *jive* means to dance to lively music.

Example: *As the yacht jibed /gybed to starboard, the bandleader gibed / jibed (mocked) the performers, who were jiving to a recording by Glenn Miller. The director's jests failed to jibe (agree) with the dancers' mood.*

hall, haul
/hôl/, /hôl/

A *hall* is a noun meaning a corridor between rooms or a large room for gatherings. *Haul* generally is a verb meaning to pull or drag. As a noun, *haul* means a long distance traveled or a stolen property.

Example: *Should I haul the box into the main hall?*

hear, here
/hir/, /hir/

Hear is a verb meaning to perceive sound. *Here* is an adverb meaning at the present place.

Example: *I hear that you were here yesterday.*

hoard, horde
/hôrd/, /hôrd/

As a verb, *hoard* means to collect or to selfishly keep, and as a noun, *hoard* means a large store of money or valuable objects. *Horde* is a noun meaning a large group of people.

Example: *A detachment from the Golden Horde discovered a hoard of gold coins in the fortress, which had been hoarded by the prior ruler.*

holey, holy, wholly
/ˈhōlē/, /ˈhōlē/, /ˈhōl(l)ē/

Holey is an adjective meaning to have holes. *Holy* is an adjective meaning sacred. *Wholly* is an adverb meaning totally or completely.

Example: *The priest's holy vestment was holey, having been wholly infested with moths over many years.*

151

ingenious, ingenuous

/inˈjēnyəs/, / ˌinˈjenyo͞oəs/

Both words are adjectives. ***Ingenious*** means clever or inventive. ***Ingenuous*** means innocent or unsuspecting.

Example: *The journeyman carpenter exercised the <u>ingenious</u> ability to use most of the scrap lumber. The <u>ingenuous</u> apprentice failed to recognize the significance of his boss's accomplishment.*

instance, instants

/ˈinstəns/, /ˈinstənts/

Both words are nouns. ***Instance*** is one event, while ***instants*** is the plural of the word *instant*, and thus means several moments of time.

Example: *During this <u>instance</u>, the conveyors experienced several <u>instants</u> of light loading.*

irrelevant, irreverent

/əˈreləvənt/, /əˈrev(ə)rənt/

Both words are adjectives. ***Irrelevant*** means not meaningful. ***Irreverent*** means disrespectful.

Example: *The supervisor made several <u>irreverent</u> remarks that were <u>irrelevant</u> to the issue.*

its, it's

/its/, /its/

Its is the possessive pronoun for the word *it*. ***It's*** is the contraction of *it is*.

Example: *<u>It's</u> time to understand <u>its</u> impact.*

know, no

/nō/, /nō/

Know is the verb meaning to understand or be acquainted with. ***No*** is the adverb or adjective meaning not.

Example: *<u>Know</u> this, when I say "<u>no</u>," I mean <u>no</u>.*

ladder, later, latter

/ˈladər/, /ˈlātər, ˈlādər/, /ˈlatər, ˈladər/

Ladder is a noun meaning a device for climbing. ***Later*** is used both as an adverb and as an adjective to mean after or following in time. ***Latter*** is an adjective meaning near to the end.

Example: *Later in the presentation, we learned how production of ladders surged in the latter months.*

lead, lead, led

/led/, /lēd/, /led/

Lead (/led/) is a noun indicating a heavy, soft, gray metal. ***Lead*** (/lēd/) is the present tense of the verb meaning go ahead while encouraging others to follow. ***Led*** (/led/) is the past tense of the verb *lead* (/lēd/) meaning to go ahead while encouraging others to follow.

Example: *Monica took the lead to eliminate lead (metal) from the chemical inventory. This led to us having more storage space.*

lessen, lesson

/ˈles(ə)n/, /ˈles(ə)n/

Lessen is a verb meaning to make less. ***Lesson*** is the noun meaning a learning experience.

Example: *The mechanic learned the lesson that he had to lessen tension on the pulley.*

loath, loathe

/lōTH, lōTH/, /lōTH/

Loath is an adjective meaning reluctant or unwilling. ***Loathe*** is a verb meaning to strongly dislike.

Example: *Sue is loath to admit that she loathes watermelon.*

loose, lose, loss

/loos/, /looz/, /lôs, läs/

Loose is an adjective meaning to be free from restraint, relaxed, or limber. ***Lose*** is a verb that means to fail to keep. ***Loss*** is a noun indicating damage or waste.

153

Example: *Be aware not to <u>lose</u> the screw. If it is too <u>loose</u>, it might vibrate <u>loose</u>, thus <u>losing</u> it and creating an even bigger <u>loss</u>.*

main, mane
/mān/, /mān/

Main is an adjective that means the most important. *Mane* is a noun that means the long hair on the neck of a horse, lion, or other animal.

Example: *The boy's <u>main</u> focus when currying (grooming) the horse was combing the <u>mane</u> and tail.*

moral, morale
/ˈmôrəl/, /məˈral/

As an adjective, *moral* means ethical or correct. As a noun, *moral* means a lesson or ethical standard. *Morale* is a noun that means the mental attitude of a person or group.

Example: *This experience cemented the well-known <u>moral</u> that <u>moral</u> behavior improves team <u>morale</u>.*

passed, past
/past/, /past/

Passed is the past tense and past participle of the verb *to pass*, which means to go by or to transmit something. As an adjective, adverb, or preposition, *past* can mean having occurred or existed in a previous time. As an adverb or preposition, *past* also can mean moving from one side to another or being later in time. As a noun, *past* means the time period before the moment of time in question or the history of a person or thing.

Example: *During the <u>past</u>, the forklift <u>passed</u> this point often. And now, I see it moving slowly <u>past</u> the garage door.*

peace, piece
/pēs/, /pēs/

Both words are nouns. *Peace* is a condition free from dissension or distraction. *Piece* is a portion of something.

Example: *Eliminating distractions proved a key <u>piece</u> to achieving <u>peace</u>.*

peak, peek, pique, piqué

/pēk/, /pēk/, /pēk/, /pēˈkā/

As a noun, *peak* means the top of a thing or the highest point. As a verb, *peak* means to reach the highest point. It also means to decline in health or spirits. In addition, as an adjective, *peak* means the greatest, best, or most. As a verb, *peek* means to look quickly; and as a noun, *peek* is the action of looking quickly. As a verb, *pique* means to stimulate interest or to be irritated by a cause. In addition, as a noun, *pique* is a feeling of irritation or resentment. Written with an acute accent mark and pronounced /pēˈkā/, *piqué* is a stiff fabric woven with a strong ribbing or raised pattern.

Example: *When John peeked out the window, he saw the tourists returning who had climbed the neighboring mountain peak. They wore red, piqué polo shirts. Their adventure piqued John's admiration, but John's son was still in a fit of pique, because he had been required to stay on the farm during the peak harvest.*

peal, peel

/pēl/, /pēl/

As a verb, *peal* means to ring loudly or make a loud sound in a manner like a bell. As a noun, *peal* is the sounding of a loud bell. As a verb, *peel* means to remove the skin of fruit, vegetables, or other similar items. As a noun, *peel* is the outer surface of fruit or vegetables.

Example: *The young woman peeled an apple while the church bells pealed.*

pedal, peddle, petal

/ˈpedl/, /ˈpedl/, /ˈpetl, ˈpedl/

As a noun, *pedal* is a foot-operated lever. As a verb, *pedal* means to move by pushing pedals, such as riding a bicycle. *Peddle* is a verb meaning to sell, especially small goods by going from place to place. A *petal* is a colored segment of a flower.

Example: *Rather than pedal his bicycle, the boy stood by the wall, awestruck by the roses with the variegated petals. Meanwhile, the street vendor continued to peddle his wares.*

pendant, pendent

/ˈpendənt/, /ˈpendənt/

Pendant is a noun meaning a piece of hanging jewelry or a hanging lamp, fan, rope, or chain. *Pendent* is an adjective meaning hanging down, pending (about to happen), or undecided.

Example: *Jacqueline remained <u>pendent</u> about her choice of a gold <u>pendant</u>.*

personal, personnel

/ˈpərs(ə)n(ə)l/, /ˌpərsəˈnel/

Personal is an adjective meaning pertaining to a particular individual. *Personnel* is a noun meaning a group of people hired to work.

Example: *She made a <u>personal</u> commitment to challenge the newly hired <u>personnel</u>.*

plain, plane

/plān/, /plān/

As an adjective, *plain* means simple, clear, or obvious. As a noun, *plain* means a flat land without trees. As a noun, *plane* is a smooth surface, either flat or sloped. In this sense, *plane* is used to describe shapes in geometry and to describe machines that fly, for example, airplanes. As a verb, *plane* means to make smooth, to fly without wing movement, or to skim over the surface of a liquid.

Example: *The plan became <u>plain</u>, as the engineer worked on the design of the <u>plane</u>. He was drafting a <u>plane</u>, which sloped at a 3.2-degree angle. Later the technician would <u>plane</u> a board to resemble the <u>plane's</u> wings.*

pole, poll

/pōl/, /pōl/

The noun *pole* is a long, slender object. As a noun, *poll* is a location where voting occurs, the process of voting, or the top of a person's head where hair grows. As a verb, *poll* means to record votes or to cut the horns off an animal, such as a cow.

Example: *While the ranchers gathered at the wooden pole, the researcher took an opinion poll by asking who preferred polled (dehorned) cattle.*

poor, pore, pour
/poor, pôr/, /pôr/, /pôr/

As an adjective, *poor* means lacking wealth or being of a low quality. As a noun, *pore* means a small opening on a surface, such as on the skin of an animal or plant. As a verb, *pore* means to think intently, such as to mentally absorb information through careful study or reading. *Pour* is a verb meaning to allow a liquid or granular substance to flow.

Example: *Sweat poured from his pores, as the poor farmer poured clover seed into the planting machine. He had pored over the question of what to do to improve the quality of his poor land.*

populace, populous
/ˈpäpyələs/, /ˈpäpyələs/

Populace is a noun meaning the people living in a place. *Populous* is an adjective meaning having a large population.

Example: *The television ad wants you to believe that the populace of London enjoys living in a populous city.*

precede, proceed
/prəˈsēd/, /prəˈsēd, prōˈsēd/

Both words are verbs. *Precede* means to come before. *Proceed* means to go forth or continue.

Example: *If we proceed with this design now, we will precede the competition.*

presence, presents
/ˈprezəns/, /prəˈzents/

As a noun, *presence* means attendance or appearance. As a verb, *presents* means to give or introduce. As a noun, the word *presents* means gifts.

Example: *Even though the handbook presents a warning about gift giving, the team leader distributed presents in the presence of the crew.*

principal, principle

/ˈprinsəpəl/, /ˈprinsəpəl/

As an adjective, *principal* means the main or most important. As a noun, *principal* means a school official, the owner or leader of a business, or a quantity of money or wealth. *Principle* is a noun meaning an important idea or truth.

Example: *The principal designer emphasized the correct engineering principles he had learned under the hands of the academy principal years before. This principle ensured the firm's principals (owners) would be protected.*

prophecy, prophesy

/ˈpräfəsē/, /ˈpräfəˌsī/

Prophecy is a noun meaning a statement about the future. *Prophesy* is a verb meaning to predict the future.

Example: *The market analysts prophesy that prices will rise. As a stockholder, I like this prophecy.*

prostate, prostrate

/ˈpräsˌtāt/, /ˈprästrāt/

Prostate is a gland in male mammals. As a verb, *prostrate* means to lie face down or to reduce someone to extreme physical weakness. As an adjective, *prostrate* means lying face down.

Example: *His father had prostate cancer. As the cancer spread to other parts of his body, it prostrated his former strength.*

quiet, quit, quite

/ˈkwīət/, /kwit/, /kwīt/

Quiet is an adjective meaning without sound. *Quit* is a verb meaning to stop. *Quite* is an adverb meaning completely or considerable.

Example: *I am quite comfortable, as long as the office is quiet. Quit disturbing me, and I will be quite happy.*

rain, reign, rein
/rān/, /rān/, /rān/

As a noun, *rain* is moisture that falls through the atmosphere. As a verb, *rain* means to fall as droplets. As a verb, *reign* means to rule as king or queen. As a noun, *reign* is the time when a king or queen rules. As a noun, *rein* is a strap attached to a bit, which is placed in an animal's mouth (especially a horse's mouth) and used to guide the animal. As a verb, *rein* means to use reins to guide or slow the movement of an animal (especially a horse). *Rein* also means to restrain anything.

Example: *During the <u>reign</u> of King Henry, it <u>rained</u> much. The severe weather <u>reined</u> in the king's military campaign.*

rational, rationale
/ˈraSH(ə)n(ə)l/, /ˌraSHəˈnal/

Rational is an adjective meaning logical. *Rationale* is a noun meaning reasons for action or belief.

Example: *The actress prided herself on being a <u>rational</u> person, and therefore she had strong <u>rationale</u> for her belief.*

respectfully, respectively
/rəˈspek(t)fəlē/, /rəˈspektivlē/

Respectfully is an adverb meaning giving respect or honor. *Respectively* is an adverb indicating the same order of items.

Example: *<u>Respectfully</u> addressing the crowd, the manager summarized the earning statement, which showed the company achieved April and May profits of $850,000 and $920,000, <u>respectively</u>.*

right, rite, write, -wright
/rīt/, /rīt/, /rīt/, /rīt/

Right is an adjective meaning correct, proper, or fair. It is also a direction, such as *right turn* or *right hand*. As a verb, *right* means to straighten, rectify, or correct. As a noun, *right* means justice or ownership. As an adverb, *right* means straight or direct, as in "*He walked <u>right</u> to his house.*" *Rite* is a noun meaning a ritual or ceremony. *Write* is a verb meaning to put words, numbers, or symbols into a record, such as *writing* on paper or *writing* an email on a computer. The suffix "*-wright*" means a worker, as in *wheelwright*.

Example: *The ship<u>wright</u> turned the drawing <u>right</u> side up. There he proceeded to <u>write</u> instructions in the <u>right</u> margin with the ferocity of a Celtic priest performing an ancient <u>rite</u>.*

segue, Segway

/ˈsegwā/, /ˈsegwā/

As a verb, *segue* means to move into another discussion topic, movie scene, or piece of music. As a noun, *segue* means an uninterrupted transition from one discussion topic, piece of music, or film scene to another. *Segway* is a trademark for a two-wheel, motorized vehicle introduced in 2001 where the rider stands directly above the axle and controls the vehicle from handles mounted on a vertical post.

Example: *The appearance of the police officer on a <u>Segway</u> gave Jane an opportunity to <u>segue</u> the conversation into another topic.*

sense, since

/sens/, /sins/

As a verb, *sense* means to feel or perceive. As a noun, *sense* is the faculty to feel or perceive. *Since* is an adverb meaning before or therefore.

Example: *They <u>sense</u> the design is correct, <u>since</u> all the pieces match. In this <u>sense</u>, they are correct. I have known this <u>since</u> yesterday.*

shone, shown

/SHōn/, /SHōn/

Shone is the past tense form of the verb *shine*, meaning to give forth light. *Shown* is the past tense form of the verb *show*, meaning to display.

Example: *Blue light <u>shone</u> from the monitor, falling across the dark room. Thus, I was <u>shown</u> the scene again.*

specie, species

/ˈspēSHē,ˈspēsē/, /ˈspēsēz,ˈspēSHēz/

Both words are nouns. *Specie* is money in the form of coins. *Species* is a group of living things capable of reproducing.

Example: *Queen Ann used <u>specie</u> to buy feathers of a beautiful <u>species</u> of parrots.*

stanch, staunch

/stôn(t)SH,stän(t)SH/, /stôn(t)SH,stän(t)SH/

Stanch is a verb meaning to stop, especially to stop the flow of blood. *Staunch* is an adjective meaning loyal or committed.

Example: *The staunch supporter of the revolution tried to stanch the continuing loss of membership from the political party.*

stationary, stationery

/ˈstāSHəˌnerē/, /ˈstāSHəˌnerē/

Stationary is an adjective meaning fixed, not moving. *Stationery* is a noun meaning paper and other materials used for writing.

Example: *The secretary stood stationary in front of the stationery store.*

steel, steal

/stēl/, /stēl/

As a noun, *steel* is a strong alloy of iron and carbon. As a verb, *steel* means to make your feelings or resolution strong. *Steal* is a verb meaning to take unlawfully. *Steal* also means to move quietly so as not to be detected.

Example: *Robbers like to steal expensive steel wheels from unprotected cars. The thieves steel their fear of being caught as they steal through the streets at night looking for targets.*

straight, strait

/strāt/, /strāt/

Straight generally is an adjective or adverb meaning staying in the same direction without bending. As a noun, *straight* means something that is free from curves or in a row (such as the *straight* in a racetrack or a *straight* in a card game like poker). As an adjective, *strait* means narrow. As a noun, *strait* means a narrow passage or situation characterized by trouble or difficulty.

Example: *After passing through the strait, Captain Magellan sailed straight northwest, because his crews were in a dire strait from a severe food shortage.*

tail, tale

/tāl/, /tāl/

Both words are nouns. *Tail* is the hindmost part of an animal, object, or group. A *tale* is a story or narrative.

Example: *The fisherman told another tale as he cut the heads and tails from the day's catch.*

tare, tear, tear

/ter/, /ter/, /tir/

As a noun, *tare* is a weed or the vetch plant, which is cultivated for fodder or silage. A *tare* also is an allowance made for the weight of a container or package when weighing an object or substance. As a verb, *tare* means to set a weighing device to accommodate the weight of a container or package. As a noun, a *tear* (/ter/), is a breach or a split, which generally damages an item. As a verb, *tear* (/ter/) means to pull apart. As a noun, a *tear* (/tir/) is a drop of liquid from in an eye. As a verb, *tear* (/tir/) means to produce tears, to cry.

Example: *The chemist knew the tare weight of the weighing dish and used this knowledge to tare the analytical scale. Later, she found a tear in her lab coat. This brought a tear to her eye.*

than, then

/THan, THən /, /THen/

Than is a conjunction or preposition used in comparisons. *Then* is an adverb that refers to time.

Example: *After removing the paper, you then can make more than a few corrections.*

their, there, they're

/THer/, /THer/, /THer/

Their is a possessive pronoun meaning belonging to persons or things. *There* is an adverb used to show an object's location. *They're* is a contraction of *they are*.

Example: *Their book is located over there, near the entrance. They're sure to find it there.*

threw, through

/THroo̅/, /THroo̅/

Threw is the past tense of the verb *throw*. ***Through*** is a preposition meaning in one end and out the other.

Example: *The motor threw a rod through the engine wall, thoroughly destroying the machine.*

to, too, two

/too̅, tə/ /too̅/, /too̅/

To is a preposition that shows movement or direction. The adverb ***too*** means also. ***Two*** is the cardinal number 2.

Example: *Sending the claim to the two companies should not be too difficult.*

venal, venial

/ˈvēnl/, /ˈvēnēəl/

Venal is an adjective meaning motivated by bribery. ***Venial*** is an adjective denoting a small sin or crime.

Example: *The venal politician was guilty of more than venial mistakes.*

veracity, voracity

/vəˈrasədē/, /vəˈrasədē/

Both words are nouns. ***Veracity*** means truthfulness. ***Voracity*** means gluttony.

Example: *The king's voracity completely discredited his veracity.*

weak, week

/wēk/, /wēk/

Weak is an adjective meaning the opposite of strong. ***Week*** is a noun meaning the length of time marked by seven days.

Example: *This activity reveals the weak link in this week's schedule.*

weather, whether

/ˈweT͟Hər/, /weT͟Hər/

As a noun, ***weather*** means the condition of the air and sky. As a verb, ***weather*** means to change or wear away do to exposure to air, rain, sunlight, and temperature change. ***Whether*** is a conjunction that introduces two or more alternatives.

Example: *Whether we understand the weather or not, we have to enjoy its variability. A wet climate can weather exposed lumber rapidly.*

whose, who's

/ho͞oz/, /ho͞oz/

Whose is a possessive pronoun meaning associated with a person. ***Who's*** is a contraction of *who is*.

Example: *Whose responsibility is it? And who's going to do something about it?*

your, you're

/yôr, yo͝or/, /yo͝or, yôr/

Your is a possessive pronoun indicating the person or persons being addressed by the speaker. ***You're*** is a contraction of *you are*.

Example: *You're correct. That is your best option.*

could of, should of, would of

Could of, ***should of***, and ***would of*** are incorrect renderings of ***could've***, ***should've***, and ***would've***, which are contractions of *could have*, *should have*, and *would have*.

Photo Credits

Page 3, Tom Peters, publicity photograph by Allison Shirreffs for Tom Peters Company, https://tompeters.com/images/reimagine/TomPeters300.jpg, accessed 13 Mar 2010, and http://www.tompeters.com/photo_credits.php, accessed 13 Mar 2010, dead URL.

Page 4, Abraham Lincoln, photograph by Alexander Gardner, 8 Nov 1863 (two weeks prior to the Gettysburg Address), Library of Congress, Prints and Photographs Division, digital ID cph.3a53289, https://commons.wikimedia.org/wiki/File:Abraham_Lincoln_head_on_s houlders_photo_portrait.jpg, accessed 22 May 2015.

Page 6, Sumerian Ur Cuneiform clay tablet, circa 2500 BC, which summarizes an account of silver, from Shuruppak or Abu Salabikh, Iraq, now at the British Museum, London, BM 15826, photograph by Gavin Collins, 27 Feb 2010, Wikimedia, https://commons.wikimedia.org/wiki/File:Sumerian_account_of_silver_f or_the_govenor.JPG, accessed 13 Oct 2018.

Page 8, Star Wars script, 3rd draft, 1 Aug 1975, photograph by Niall Balmer, http://www.originalstarwarsprops.com/episodeiv.htm, accessed 22 May 2015, dead URL. Used by written permission.

Page 29, Ralph Waldo Emerson, photograph by Southworth & Hawes, circa 1857, George Eastman House Collection, Accession Number: 1981:2711:0001, https://commons.wikimedia.org/wiki/File:Ralph_Waldo_Emerson_ca185 7.jpg, accessed 22 May 2015.

Page 44, James Thurber, publicity photograph published 1935, by Harper & Brothers, Library of Congress, Prints and Photographs division, reproduction number LC USZ62-127411, call number NYWTS - BIOG--Thurber, James, online catalog https://www.loc.gov/pictures/item/2001695413/, widely published on the internet, accessed 22 May 2015.

Page 52, Ernest Hemingway, editing at desk at Sun Valley Lodge, Idaho, Dec 1939, publicity photograph by Lloyd Arnold for Charles Scribner's Sons, City of Toronto Archives, fonds 1244, William James family fonds, item 2111, http://www1.toronto.ca/City%20Of%20Toronto/City%20Clerks/Toronto

%20Archives/Images/f1244_it2111.jpg, accessed 27 May 2015, dead URL. As of 2015, the Toronto Archives catalog mistakenly attributed the date to circa 1930, but the date is from 1939; the photograph closely resembles a similar publicity photograph taken by Lloyd Arnold for the dust jacket of the first edition of *For Whom the Bell Tolls*, https://commons.wikimedia.org/wiki/File:ErnestHemingway.jpg, accessed 27 May 2015.

Notes

[1] Tom Peters, "Brand You Thoughts from Tom Peters: Work on Your Writing," YouTube video, Tom Peters channel, uploaded 21 Jan 2010, https://youtu.be/EEHLHdoPfWA, accessed 3 Oct 2018.

[2] Wikipedia, "Gettysburg Address," https://en.wikipedia.org/wiki/Gettysburg_Address, accessed 3 Oct 2018.

[3] Marvin H. Swift, "Clear Writing Means Clear Thinking Means…," *Harvard Business Review*, Jan 1973; modified version online at https://hbr.org/1973/01/clear-writing-means-clear-thinking-means, accessed 3 Oct 2018.

[4] Radicati Group (technology market research firm), "Email Statistics Report, 2015-2019," no date, https://www.radicati.com/wp/wp-content/uploads/2015/02/Email-Statistics-Report-2015-2019-Executive-Summary.pdf, accessed 17 Jul 2020; "Email Market, 2018-2022," Radicati Group, Mar 2018, summarized by Heinz Tschabitscher, in "The Number of Emails Sent Per Day in 2018," Lifewire (company that provides content regarding electronic technology), https://www.lifewire.com/how-many-emails-are-sent-every-day-1171210, accessed 9 Sep 2018, article at URL subsequently was changed. In addition, Andrea Robbins, "The Shocking Truth about How Many Emails Are Sent," Campaign Monitor (email marketing company), 19 Mar 2018, https://www.campaignmonitor.com/blog/email-marketing/2018/03/shocking-truth-about-how-many-emails-sent/, accessed 3 Oct 2018, dead URL.

[5] Although often attributed to Mark Twain, no one knows who first made this statement; Wikiquote, "Mark Twin," https://en.wikiquote.org/wiki/Mark_Twain, accessed 3 Oct 2018.

[6] OCLC, "Inside World Cat," https://www.oclc.org/en/worldcat/inside-worldcat.html, accessed 10 Jul 2020.

[7] Although widely quoted on the internet and attributed to Ralph Waldo Emerson, the passage is not traceable to any actual source and not present on any of the online sites that quote Emerson.

[8] Roger Angell, Forward to *The Elements of Style*, by William Struck Jr. and E. B. White (Longman imprint, Pearson Education Company, 4th edition, 2000), p. ix.

[9] William Stafford, as quoted by Steven Ratiner, in *Giving Their Word: Conversations With Contemporary Poets* (University of Massachusetts

Press, 2002), p. 19, online at
https://books.google.com/books?id=RLxZAAAAMAAJ&q=%22Lower+
your+standards+and+keep+writing%22&dq=%22Lower+your+standards
+and+keep+writing%22&ei=5ZUzS8XeEKHiyQSr9a2tAQ&cd=1,
accessed 3 Oct 2018.

[10] James Thurber, "The Sheep in Wolf's Clothing," *The New Yorker,*
29 Apr 1939, and *Fables for Our Time & Famous Poems Illustrated,*
1940, as quoted by Wikiquote, in "James Thurber,"
https://en.wikiquote.org/wiki/James_Thurber, accessed 15 Jul 2015.

[11] Ray Bradbury, "A Conversation with Ray Bradbury," a short film by
Lawrence Bridges, produced by the National Endowment for the Arts for
the Big Read program, YouTube video, TheRedCarChannel channel,
uploaded 11 Sep 2008, https://youtu.be/EzD0YtbViCs, accessed 3 Oct
2018; 3½ minutes into the video Bradbury describes his writing at the
University of California, Los Angeles (UCLA) library. The Larry
Bridges channel uploaded to YouTube on 8 Jul 2009 a longer version of
the interview, https://youtu.be/PF3uZf4G3Lo, accessed 3 Oct 2018.

[12] For instance, see Laurence O'Donnell, "Music and the Brain,"
http://www.cerebromente.org.br/n15/mente/musica.html, accessed 3 Oct
2018, and Arthur Harvey, "An Intelligence View of Music Education,"
http://webshare.northseattle.edu/fam180/topics/music/musicand%20mind
.htm, accessed 3 Oct 2018, dead URL.

[13] Ernest Hemingway, *Moveable Feast: The Restored Edition* (Scribner,
2014), p. 26.

[14] Father Tom Allender, S. J., quoted by Scott Wood in "Sharpening
Your Legal Writing Skills," which appeared in "Survival Guide for New
Attorneys in California," *Los Angeles Lawyer*, (Los Angeles County Bar
Association magazine), Fall 2006, p. 9-10,
https://www.lacba.org/docs/default-source/lal-back-issues/2006-
issues/survival-guide-fall-2006.pdf, accessed 3 Oct 2018.

[15] Richard Lederer, *The Miracle of Language* (Simon and Schuster, 1991,
revised 1999), p. 30-31; also online at
http://verbivore.com/wordpress/the-case-for-the-strength-and-grace-of-
short-words/, accessed 3 Oct 2018.

[16] John Dewey, *The Quest for Certainty* (George Allen & Unwin Ltd.,
London, 1929), p. 120, online at
https://archive.org/details/questforcertaint029410mbp/page/n125,
accessed 3 Oct 2018.

[17] This example uses common environmental abbreviations: FA = federal action, EIS = environmental impact statement, EA = environmental assessment, NSI = no significant impact, LA = lead agency, FONSI = finding of no significant impact, PA = proposed action, and CATEX = categorical exclusion.

[18] Avi Selk, "One space between each sentence, they said. Science just proved them wrong." *The Washington Post*, 4 May 2018, https://www.washingtonpost.com/news/speaking-of-science/wp/2018/05/04/one-space-between-each-sentence-they-said-science-just-proved-them-wrong-2/, accessed 22 Nov 2018; and Rebecca L. Johnson, Becky Bui, and Lindsay L. Schmitt, "Are two spaces better than one? The effect of spacing following periods and commas during reading," *Attention, Perception, & Psychophysics*, Vol. 80, p. 1504-1511, published 24 Apr 2018, issued Aug 2018, https://link.springer.com/article/10.3758/s13414-018-1527-6, accessed 17 Jul 2020.

[19] Steve Rayson, "We Analyzed 100 Million Headlines. Here's What We Learned (New Research)," BuzzSumo (social media metrics company), 26 Jun 2017, https://buzzsumo.com/blog/most-shared-headlines-study/, accessed 20 May 2019, title subsequently changed; and Simon Edelstyn, employee of Outbrain (content distribution and monitoring company), "5 Tips to Help Improve Your Headline Click-Through Rate," *The Guardian*, 28 Mar 2013, content provided by Outbrain, http://www.theguardian.com/media-network-outbrain-partner-zone/5-tips-headline-click-through-rate, accessed circa 2013, dead URL, copy at https://web.archive.org/web/20131205105615/http://www.theguardian.com/media-network-outbrain-partner-zone/5-tips-headline-click-through-rate, accessed 20 May 2019. Also see Kevan Lee, "Infographic: The Optimal Length for Every Social Media Update and More," Buffer (social media management company), 21 Oct 2014, revised 30 Nov 2018, https://buffer.com/library/optimal-length-social-media, accessed 20 May 2019.

[20] Jeffrey Kuiken, Anne Schuth, Martijn Spitters, and Maarten Marx, "Effective Headlines of Newspaper Articles in a Digital Environment," *Digital Journalism* (journal published by Taylor & Francis academic press), on 2 Feb 2017, vol. 5, issue 10, p. 1300-1314, https://www.tandfonline.com/doi/full/10.1080/21670811.2017.1279978, accessed 20 May 2019.

[21] D. Bnonn Tennant, "Can You Write a Better Headline Than This? Not Using Old Headline Formulas You Can't," KissMetrics (social media

company), circa 19 Dec 2011, http://blog.kissmetrics.com/how-to-write-headlines/, accessed 2013, dead URL, copy at https://web.archive.org/web/20120107151230/https://blog.kissmetrics.com/how-to-write-headlines/, accessed 20 May 2019; and Jakob Nielson, "First 2 Words: A Signal for the Scanning Eye," Nielsen Norman Group (computer interface consulting firm), 6 Apr 2009, https://www.nngroup.com/articles/first-2-words-a-signal-for-scanning/, accessed 20 May 2019.

Index

Author

Charles Maxwell is an engineer, financial analyst, and manager in the mining industry. In addition to advancing projects and evaluating acquisitions, he ghostwrites memoirs and teaches business writing and financial analysis.

If you have a compelling story to tell or you need to elevate the writing skills at your organization, contact him at: www.ToweringSkills.com/contact/.

If you are interested in buying 10 or more copies of this book, contact us for a discount schedule at: www.ToweringSkills.com/contact/.

One Last Thing

If this book helped you, please post a review on Amazon.

Made in the USA
Columbia, SC
23 August 2024

41004909R00102